KANSAS CITY
BARBEQUE

**From the Kansas City
Barbeque Inner Circle**

Bill Venable

Rick Welch

Bruce Daniel

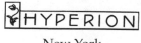

HYPERION

New York

The phrase "If it doesn't move too quickly, it ends up great on a grill" is heard often in Kansas City, typifying the prevailing barbeque attitude: Any and all foods can benefit from Kansas City-style preparation.

Kansas City barbeque has several distinctive features. First, marinades and/or rubs are used for both their tenderizing and flavor-enhancing traits. Next, cooking is done over wood fires, most often hickory or hickory blends to provide a smokey, distinctive nuance. When ready for serving, a rich, sweet-hot tomato and molasses-based sauce is applied, or served on the side. For many, the mix of flavors imparted by marinades, rubs, and wood smoke are sufficiently satisfying: for others, a K.C. sauce-style is the perfect final touch to an already exceptional barbeque experience.

Copyright © 1993, 1996, River City Products, Inc.

KANSAS CITY BARBEQUE is a revised edition of
ABSOLUTE BARBEQUE, previously published
by Old Market Press.
Original Recipes by: Bill Venable and Rick Welch
Edited by: Bill Venable, Rick Welch, and Bruce Daniel

Library of Congress Cataloging-in-Publication Data
Kansas City barbeque : over 125 of the best recipes for charcoal
and gas grills by America's premier barbeque experts / Kansas City
Barbeque Inner Circle.
        p.   cm.
    Includes index.
    ISBN 0-7868-8171-2
    1. Barbeque cookery.   I. Kansas City Barbeque Inner Circle
(Group)
TX840.B3K36   1996
641.5'784 — dc20   96–33955
                                                       CIP

FIRST EDITION

10 9 8 7 6 5 4 3 2 1

Contents

Extended Excellence—2nd Degree Specialties 77

Lengthy Leisure—3rd Degree Specialties 105

Introduction

In Kansas City, barbeque had always been part of the culture. While other areas of the country do barbeque, none has as many good barbeque restaurants (over 70 are listed in the Yellow Pages) or has as wide a range of barbequed foods. The city's populace takes tremendous pride in the worldwide recognition it has received for its barbeque prowess. Additionally, Kansas Citians are rabid outdoor chefs prone to compete for the honor of being the best barbequer on the block. Kansas City barbeque deserves the recognition it has received because the food has become both an art form and a revered tradition. Virtually all Kansas Citians have informed, experience-driven opinions on barbeque. This knowledge, which is the result of having enjoyed a multitude of barbequed masterpieces (from both restaurants and backyard smokers), eventually leads to a conclusion that is both natural and unquestioned:

No place approaches Kansas City when it comes to barbeque excellence.

Numerous factors have contributed to making Kansas City the world's barbeque mecca:

- Kansas City has been a livestock center for over a century.
- Being centrally located, Kansas City has become a true crossroads of grilling and smoking techniques.
- Hardwoods of many types are available locally, thus allowing for a myriad of subtle smoke methods and flavors.
- As Kansas City has become well known for its barbeque, the competition to create ever-better flavors and techniques has steadily increased at both the home and restaurant level.

Kansas City became a livestock center during the late 1800s, and by the early years of the twentieth century several barbeque "joints" appeared, attempting not only to take advantage of Kansas City steaks (which were without equal), but to find ways to successfully prepare other cuts. Slow smoking techniques were developed as an effort to "dress up" inexpensive meats. Eventually, grilling and smoking methods were applied to the extensive mix of livestock available to the area, and now, decades later, the experience and innovation typical of Kansas City has resulted in the ultimate in barbeque, characterized by uniform excellence with unequalled diversity.

The phrase "If it doesn't move too quickly, it ends up great on a grill" is heard often in Kansas City, typifying the prevailing barbeque attitude: Any and all foods can benefit from Kansas City-style preparation.

Kansas City barbeque has several distinctive features. First, marinades and/or rubs are used for both their tenderizing and flavor enhancing traits. Next, cooking is done over wood fires, most often hickory or hickory blends to provide a smoky, distinctive nuance. When ready for serving, a rich, sweet-hot tomato and molasses-based sauce is applied, or served on the side. For many, the mix of flavors imparted by marinades, rubs, and wood smoke are sufficiently satisfying; for others, a K.C.-style sauce is the perfect final touch to an already exceptional barbeque experience.

The goal of this book is simple: to enable the user to create excellent barbeque dishes. Whether you are a grill novice or an experienced chef, the recipes and techniques outlined within this book will be of value to you. Icons offered for each recipe allow for easy selection based on type and time available. The methods described, equipment recommended, and techniques provided are based on the solid barbeque experience of the Kansas City Barbeque Inner Circle.

Inner Circle membership is by invitation only. Those within the Inner Circle have distinguished themselves by winning awards in numerous regional and national barbeque competitions, founding barbeque organizations, owning barbeque businesses, and creating barbeque publications and products.

The extensive expertise within the Inner Circle, conveyed throughout this book, will enable you to achieve excellence both in grilling and smoking simply and consistently.

Absolute Barbeque

We all know the feeling. That wonderful aroma has been in the air for just long enough. The conversation has been good, the beverages refreshing. But an expectant nerve twitch has been egged on, hour upon hour, by the anticipation, the hankering, for what's right over there in the smoker.

The host has been cordial, but it's getting hard to wait another minute because the entire atmosphere, delicately laced with smoke and camaraderie, has made everyone's palate insistent and demanding, desirous of that foremost expression of smoke—barbeque expertly prepared, bursting with flavor and sensual delight. The entire scenario is making everyone wild about barbeque!!!

Ravenous, insatiable guests about to pounce! Unchecked, this is what it comes to: *Adults unable to help themselves. The allure of the smoke, the call of the "Q." Passion in need of an outlet. . .* Absolute Barbeque is not an overstatement. Anyone fortunate enough to have partaken of truly transcendental smoked goods has been marked for life, and what forms does this wildness take? Why so wild about Absolute Barbeque?

Because barbeque is versatile.

The various items in this tome range from simple to complex. The settings for such culinary delights can be casual or elegant. The audience for these dishes is unbounded by age, background, or social status. Barbeque appeals to everyone.

Because barbeque is functional.

The techniques used herein enable the user to create exquisite results from anything. Originally conceived as a way to "make do" with whatever was available, barbeque became an art form as marinades, rubs, spices, and smoke enhanced any and all cuts of meat.

Because barbeque is an event.

Without barbeque, how could one even relate to the Fourth of July? Would Memorial Day, Father's Day, and Labor Day approximate their fond hold on our imaginations were it not for barbeque? Indeed, do not the ritual and ceremony involved in the bond of barbeque make it a uniting force for family and friends? Such is the strength of "Q."

Because barbeque is personal.

True devotees of the grill are as proud of their efforts as any artist or craftsman. The long hours spent tending fires are borne out of a sense of passion for their creations. The satisfaction experienced by chef and guest are bonds that are not to be taken lightly.

Because barbeque is American.

No form of cooking is so identifiably American as the backyard barbeque. Nothing else even comes close.

Absolute Barbeque

In many ways an understatement, our appreciation for this heartfelt and uniquely American art form stems from a belief that barbecuing is an ideal way to spend time with friends and family, to explore new techniques in an exceptionally personal form of expression, and to enjoy the myriad aromas, textures, and flavors inherent in barbeque's rich and varied world.

The Three Degrees
of Barbeque

This book employs a degree system, which groups recipes based on the amount of time involved during the barbecuing process. This arrangement makes it simple to select the pork, beef, poultry, lamb, sausage, or seafood technique that best suits your time frame.

1ST DEGREE selections are generally completed in fifteen minutes to one hour. These are grilling techniques done over high heat. This quick-preparation section—"Punctual Perfection"—allows for all the sensory delights of true barbeque, yet accomplishes it in a short amount of time. A quickie unequaled.

2ND DEGREE creations—"Extended Excellence"—are affairs drawn out over more time, say two to four hours, where temperatures are lower and smoking is done in a covered unit. This section allows ample time to enjoy various other pleasures as smoke aroma pervades the senses.

3RD DEGREE efforts—"Lengthy Leisure"—are for those willing to put in a minimum of five hours in pursuit of the barbeque ideal. Some of these recipes, ambitious to the hilt, take upwards of fifteen hours, since large cuts require lots of slow-smoke time. But, as true barbeque warlords will attest, time spent barbecuing is a ritualistic reverie of the first magnitude, and worth every minute.

It is important to indicate here that the progression through 1st, 2nd, and 3rd Degree recipes is simply a function of time. The recipes are not necessarily any more complex or difficult in later sections, but they will take longer to complete for Absolute Barbeque Perfection.

The Basics of Barbeque:
Learning to Control the Elements

Cremated outside, raw inside.
Totally torched.
Dry and brittle.
Underdone and scary-looking.
Tastes like lighter fluid.
Looks like a penny loafer.

If you're lucky, you've somehow avoided all that's just been mentioned, but odds are you've had to endure backyard barbeque disasters when someone's good intentions fell well short of perfection. This book is designed to help you avoid all of the mistakes listed above by making grilling and smoking simple and enjoyable.

The Elements of Barbeque
Your Keys to Great Results

Controlling the four basic elements in barbecuing assures good results. The following is a typical scenario that outlines the proper way to (1) construct a fire, (2) control moisture, and (3) impart flavor. Element (4), time, becomes a product of the other three elements, as we will see.

Element One: Fire. Wood, charcoal, or gas fires work well. Charcoal should be allowed to form a thin white ash before the cooking process begins.

If simply grilling, the coals should be spread out evenly with the grill three to five inches above the fire. Use of wood chips is optional.

When smoking, the fire should not be directly under the meat. Using indirect heat lowers the temperature and allows use of water pans and drip pans. Set the cooking surface up as far from the fire as possible.

Element Two: Moisture. The retention and addition of moisture are necessary components of the smoking art. They can be accomplished by basting the entree of choice or using a water pan. Using soaked wood chunks or chips can help as well.

Element Three: Woods. The smoke flavor imparted by good, seasoned wood gives barbeque its uniqueness. Many chefs build their fires solely with flavored woods; others place soaked chunks or chips on charcoal or gas fires. Either method works well. Oak, hickory, apple, cherry, pecan—these and various other woods are all sworn to be the best, depending on the chef and what is being prepared.

Element Four: Time. This element can last minutes or hours depending on the control of the other three elements and the size and type of cut to be cooked. Thus, the suggested time for any recipe depends on the control of fire and moisture, combined with outdoor conditions.

Control of the elements requires some experimentation and magic. A proper fire, adequate moisture, flavorful wood—all will give good results. But other essentials aid in the preparation of mind-boggling barbeque, and that's what we'll discuss next.

Secrets Shared:
Easy Techniques to Make YOUR Barbeque Exquisite

The following suggestions have been assembled from the combined knowledge of countless contest winners, product manufacturers, and barbeque titans whose sentiments generally flow along similar lines. In no particular order, these tips will allow for your complete and resounding barbeque success:

- Familiarize yourself totally with your equipment.
- Buy a real thermometer (don't trust any thermometer that comes on a smoker), and put it up by the top vents. When the temperature drops 20 to 25 degrees, add a handful of briquettes and some wood.
- Open the bottom vents fully and control heat with top ones.
- Indirect Cooking: With this technique the grill is divided into two parts. There is a searing side and a cooking side. This is achieved by placing the charcoal briquettes off to one side over which the meat can be seared to seal in juices and moisture. Once seared, the meat is cooked on the indirect side of the grill. Cooking is done away from the charcoal giving you more control over more even heat. This provides two things, a slower cooking time without burning the food, and less opportunity for grease fires from juices that would otherwise fall directly upon the briquettes.
- Smoking: Building upon the indirect method described above, smoking is done over low heat between 200 and 225 degrees in a covered unit. Things cook more slowly, mois-

ture is essential to the process, and smoke flavor is imparted from selected woods.

The fire will be added to in equal amounts of charcoal and wood at regular intervals. You will also have a water source, a metal pan, near the fire, and directly under the item you are smoking. The water source will keep moisture in the cooking unit. The moisture will blend with the smoke and heat to add true barbeque flavor to your efforts.

- Make notes on what works and what needs to be tried the next time. Don't trust your memory.
- Use marinades or rubs (dry spices rubbed into the meat) whenever barbecuing.
- Apply sauce only after the meat is off the grill, or have it on the side, or don't use it at all (if the marinade and/or rub has done its job properly).
- Use a clean cooker every time—there's a definite difference in taste.
- Use hickory sparingly—it can be overpowering and bitter.
- Make sure any wood used is well seasoned.
- Slow cooking is always preferred.
- While grocery-store charcoal is acceptable, lump hardwood charcoal (made from wood with a minimum of fillers) is preferable since it burns hotter, longer, and cleaner.
- Let anything that is destined for the grill or smoker reach room temperature first. Do not start with cold meat.
- Accessories: Many of the following items make successful barbeque easier and allow for more versatility.

Basting brush
Tongs
Apron
Mitt
Wire brush for grill cleaning
Charcoal chimney for quick-starting briquettes
Spray bottle for any flareups
Water pan(s)
Rotisserie
Rib racks
Long-handled spatula
Drip pan
Starters (solid/liquid/electric)

Secrets of the Gas Grill

Within this section are detailed the secrets of the gas grill. In recent years, the popularity of the gas grill has increased dramatically. Currently, more of them are being sold than conventional charcoal grills. This trend confirms the reality in many households: time is short, gas grills are quick.

The Kansas City Barbeque Inner Circle continually updates its thinking and techniques to include all manner of barbeque devotees. Though purists within our ranks have sometimes spoken unkindly of gas grills, we now recognize their importance. Indeed, gas grills often provide advantages over other types of grilling and smoking units.

Gas grills equal speed. They are ready to go as soon as they are lit, unlike charcoal or wood fires which take a minimum of twenty minutes until they are just right.

Gas grills offer consistency. Once the flame level is set, constant temperature is maintained. And since constant temperature is essential to real barbeque success, the gas grill has a clear advantage in this area.

Gas grills have become much more wide-ranging in their capabilities. The better gas grills on the market today have features that enable them to compete successfully with conventional grills and smokers.

Gas grills now have multiple burners, allowing for indirect cooking. This is great for steaks, where searing can be done over direct heat, after which the meat can be placed over indirect heat for finishing. Cuts requiring lower temperatures or longer cooking times can benefit from the indirect method as well.

Many of the newer gas grill models have steamer compartments and/or built-in grids for delicate items such as seafood and vegetables. For models without such features, equivalent accessories are readily available and affordable.

Smoke flavor can be introduced through the use of wood chip containers available as inexpensive accessories. By using these devices, the backyard chef can impart smoke flavor quickly and easily.

Moisture (needed in longer cooking/smoking efforts) can be effectively included in the gas grill process by simply placing a pan of water on or over the heat source.

A Fine Balance Maintained

As mentioned in previous sections, truly tasty barbeque is the result of the proper combination of the basic elements: time, temperature, smoke, and moisture. The good news is that gas grills can be just as effective in attaining the correct balance of these elements as conventional units.

A few things to keep in mind:

Grilling on a gas unit is essentially the same as grilling over wood or charcoal fires.

If you haven't already, really familiarize yourself with your grill. Understand it. Your results will be enhanced.

When cooking covered (smoking), gas grills differ from conventional units. Wood or charcoal gives off water molecules as well as heat. Gas units do not. Because they don't, adding a pan of water on or over the heat source will provide necessary moisture.

Gas Grill Applications in This Edition

The first two sections of this book ("Appetizers" and "Punctual Perfection—1st Degree Specialties") are ideal for the gas grill user. All the recipes are to be done over high heat for short periods of time with a minimum of smoke flavor.

The remaining sections ("2nd" and "3rd Degree Specialties") work well for the gas grill as long as indirect heat, a water source, and smoke flavor are provided. The only necessary reminder for longer efforts is to make sure there is sufficient gas for the cooking times required. Running out of fuel halfway through is undesirable, to say the least.

In modern life the gas grill is essential. Nobody has time anymore. Technology's much hoped-for ability to lessen work loads and provide additional leisure time has not yet come to pass.

Do you remember when the future had "paperless" offices where machines did the work as individuals calmly dictated appropriate tasks?

Do you remember hearing about the impressive amount of additional personal time one would have, in the future, to explore the human experience more fully?

Do you remember when technology was going to eliminate the mundane and the repetitive?

- The machine to automatically mow the lawn!
- A robot to clean the house!
- Off to vacation destinations on automated skyways!

Do you remember the future? It still has not arrived.

At the end of the workday, beleaguered and bedraggled, we leave unpaperless work-filled businesses, only to confront the next dilemma: What's for supper??

Thinking quickly, options arise:

- Yet another trip to a too-familiar fast-food chain?
- Maybe it's time to blow a week's wages at some over-priced bistro featuring art-food mini-portions.
- How about hunkering down at the local pub & grub for some calorie-laden heavy fuel offerings?
- Or perhaps the watering hole where everybody already knows too much about you?

Do yourself a favor instead. Consult the quick-preparation sections of this book for exciting, easily grilled masterpieces. In less than an hour, a wonderful, healthy meal can be created and enjoyed using nothing more than a gas grill and the techniques described herein.

For those short on time, this book has THE quick-preparation answers.

Symbols of Success

The Symbols of Success chart below depicts three elements critical to your barbeque success—time, temperature, and smoke. The correct mix of these is found on each page of and each recipe has its optimum formula illustrated.

As you can see, the illustration below calls for three hours of cooking at a low, slow temperature, with slight smoke flavor.

This scientific application of the basic barbeque art is an "Inner Circle" first. A brief explanation of these elements follows.

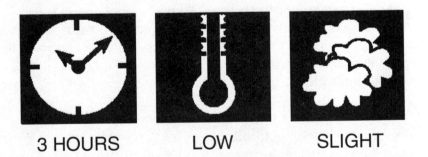

| 3 HOURS | LOW | SLIGHT |

Time

Time relates directly to the type and amount of food being cooked.

Temperature

Temperature varies with cooking time, with the hottest fires used for the shortest cooking, cooler fires for slow smoking. (See temperature gauge at top of page xxv.)

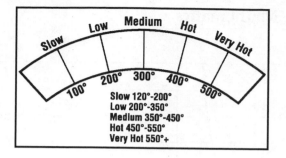

Slow 120°-200°
Low 200°-350°
Medium 350°-450°
Hot 450°-550°
Very Hot 550°+

Smoke

Smoke permeates the meat over time, giving it the distinctive flavor of the type of wood being used.

The basic barbeque elements relate in ways that the Inner Circle further illustrates on the page opposite—Barbeque Mathematics. The Symbols of Success chart on each recipe page, as in the illustration on page xxiv, is a "snapshot" of a point on the Barbeque Mathematics graph.

Gas Grill

This symbol indicates recipes that are well suited for preparation on a gas grill. While such recipes can be prepared on either a gas grill or with a conventional unit, those with this symbol are grilled rapidly with a minimum of smoke flavor.

Fish and seafood are ideal for the gas grill since they require short cooking times over high heat. Since large fish require only 8 to 10 minutes per pound and fillets need only 5 minutes per side, fish and seafood are gas grill naturals.

Any of the recipes in the 1st Degree section may be used on a gas grill. Numerous 2nd Degree recipes lend themselves to gas grill cooking and are appropriately noted. 3rd Degree recipes are not recommended for preparation on a gas grill since the advantages of a gas grill (higher heat, not a lot of smoke requirements) decrease the long cooking times.

Barbeque Mathematics

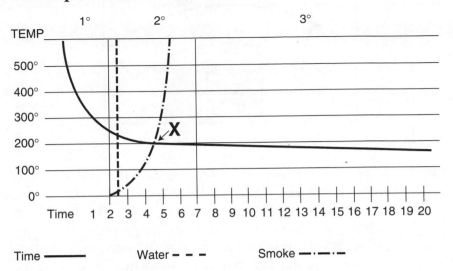

Do not be scared by the graph on this page! Conceived in a bar-beque-addled moment of transcendent inspiration, it shows how the elements of barbeque relate!

Time stretches out from left to right along the baseline, and corresponds to 1st, 2nd, and 3rd Degree sections in the book.

Temperature rises up the left side of the graph.

Smoke is imparted over time. Notice how the temperature curve drops with time as the smoke curve rises.

The Inner Circle knows that each and every recipe contained in this book falls at some point within the graph above, contain-ing just the right amount of each barbeque element. And with a Symbols of Success chart depicting an exact point from the Barbeque Mathematics graph, the proper mix of elements is insured on each recipe.

The "X" on the graph shows the exact point for the Symbols of Success chart shown on page xxiv.

With Barbeque Mathematics and Symbols of Success, the Inner Circle has explained the "scientific" elements of world-class barbeque. The recipes themselves, along with your own personal flair, provide the final magic that results in the sensory thrills of barbeque perfectly prepared.

All These Words Are Causing HUNGER!
Let's Cook Something!

An Easy Smoked Sausage Technique to Get You Started:

1. Allow sausage (let's try 5 pounds or so of mild or hot Italian, long and coiled) to reach room temperature.
2. Mound 20 to 25 hardwood charcoal briquettes on one side of the fire grate in your smoker (or prepare a like amount in a charcoal chimney). Start the fire. On a gas grill, light one side only.
3. When the coals are white, add pre-moistened wood chips or chunks (whatever type you choose). Don't spread the coals out as you would for grilling: leave them pretty well piled up on one side so that you can place the meat opposite, not above, the fire. Add a water pan if desired.
4. Place the sausage on the grill away from the fire, have the bottom vents wide open, close the lid.
5. Monitor the temperature in the smoker and adjust it to 200-220 degrees by opening/closing the top-side vents, or by adjusting the flame on the gas grill. Once this temperature is reached, the only reason to open the lid is to add more briquettes/wood (if temperature drops 20-25 degrees), in conventional units. Some smoke should be wafting out of the unit at all times.
6. Continue to monitor the temperature, turn the sausage a time or two, add fuel if necessary. And an hour to an hour and a half later, pull it out, add some sauce if you feel like it, and have a smoked sausage feast!

This same technique would work for chicken pieces (you might want to marinate the chicken and baste during smoking), or a small pork tenderloin (with which you might want to use a good basic rub).

Use your imagination with woods, marinades, rubs, and spices, all of which are outlined in the recipes that follow.

Beginnings
of the
Perfect BBQ

APPETIZERS

Chinese Fire Drill Beef Strips

1 pound beef fillet or tenderloin
1/2 cup soy sauce
1 clove garlic, pressed
1 teaspoon ground ginger

Cut the meat into thin strips. Mix the soy sauce, garlic, and ginger and pour over the beef strips. Let marinate for about 1 hour. Meanwhile, soak small bamboo skewers in water for a half hour or longer.

Prepare a wood or charcoal fire or preheat a gas grill. Thread the beef on the skewers and grill 1 minute on each side over a hot fire. Baste with remaining marinade after turning.

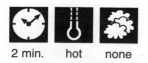

2 min.   hot   none

Fiesta Livers

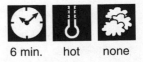

1 pound chicken livers
1 cup Madeira
1 tablespoon garlic salt
Freshly ground pepper to taste
2 tablespoons butter or vegetable oil
Bacon strips

Marinate the livers for 2 hours in a mixture of Madeira, garlic salt, and pepper. Meanwhile, soak 8- or 10-inch wooden skewers in water.

Drain the livers and sauté them in the butter for several minutes; allow to cool. Wrap each liver in a bacon strip, threading 4 livers to a bamboo skewer.

Prepare a wood or charcoal fire or preheat a gas grill. Cook the livers over a hot fire, turning frequently and watching to control flare-ups from the dripping bacon fat. Grill until the bacon is crisp, about 6 minutes.

6 min.   hot   none

Backyard Grilled Spiced Shrimp

1 pound shrimp
1 stick butter or margarine
2 tablespoons Backyard BBQ & Grill Seasoning
1 can beer

Soak 8- or 10-inch bamboo skewers in water for a half hour or more. Prepare a wood or charcoal fire or a gas grill.

Shell and devein the shrimp. Thread 5 or 6 shrimp on each well-soaked bamboo skewer. Melt the butter and stir in the BBQ & Grill Seasoning or a spicy rub of your choice. Brush the shrimp with the spiced butter and grill over a hot fire until pink, about 5 to 7 minutes, while continuing to brush with butter. If flames should erupt, douse with beer and apply more butter.

Backyard BBQ & Grill Seasoning

If unavailable in your area, you can create your own mixture. Combine 1 part paprika, 1 part ground black pepper, and 1 part salt. Mix a large batch and use as needed with your favorite backyard recipes.

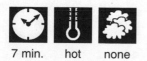

7 min.   hot   none

Grilled Mussels au Shroom

24 large mussels
1 cup white wine
1 cup water
1 tablespoon butter or margarine
24 mushroom caps
24 (2-inch) bacon strips
1/2 cup flour
2 eggs, beaten
1/2 cup olive oil
1/4 cup minced parsley
2 cloves garlic, pressed

Put some 10-inch bamboo skewers in water to soak while you prepare the mussels.

Scrub the mussels with a stiff brush under cold running water and pull or cut off the beards. Place the mussels in a kettle and add 2/3 cup of boiling water. Return to a boil, cover tightly, and steam for 3 minutes, until the shells open. (Discard any mussels that do not open.) Shuck the mussels and pat dry with paper towels.

Combine the wine, water, and butter in a medium saucepan, bring to a boil, and add the mushroom caps. Simmer for 2 to 3 minutes. Drain and allow to cool slightly.

Thread the mussels, mushrooms, and bacon alternately on the skewers. Dust them with flour, dip in the beaten egg, and roll in bread crumbs. Refrigerate while you prepare a basting sauce by beating together the oil, parsley, and garlic.

Prepare a wood or charcoal fire or preheat a gas grill until hot. Grill the mussels on one side for 5 minutes, basting often. Turn and baste the other side for about 5 minutes longer, until golden brown.

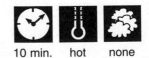

10 min.   hot   none

Waddle's Magic Meatballs

1 pound ground sirloin
1 egg
Pimiento-stuffed green olives, drained
Salt and pepper
Garlic powder
Olive oil
Parsley flakes

Soak some 8- or 10-inch bamboo skewers in water for half an hour or more. Prepare a wood or charcoal fire or preheat a gas grill.

Put the ground beef and egg in a mixing bowl and sprinkle with salt, pepper, and garlic powder to taste. Mix well. Mold some of the meat mixture around an olive to make a meatball twice the size of the olive. Repeat until all the meat mixture is used.

Brush the meatballs with olive oil and roll in parsley. Place on skewers, allowing 4 meatballs per skewer, and grill over a hot fire, turning occasionally, for about 10 minutes or until browned.

Remove from the skewers onto a platter and serve hot as hors d'oeuvres.

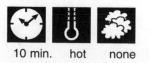

10 min.　　hot　　none

Mama's Italian Sausage Poppers

1/2 pound Italian sausage, casings removed
1/2 pound cooked ham
1/2 pound hard salami
1/4 cup parsley flakes
1 teaspoon crushed oregano
1/4 cup minced onion
1 tablespoon lemon juice
1/2 pound sliced lean bacon

Begin soaking some 8- to 10-inch wooden skewers in water while you prepare a wood or charcoal fire or preheat a gas grill.

Combine the sausage, ham, and salami in a food processor. Chop fine. Add the parsley, oregano, onion, and lemon juice. Mix thoroughly. Form the mixture into 1-inch balls and wrap with bacon strips. Place 3 balls on each skewer and grill over a hot fire for about 9 minutes, turning often, until the bacon is crisp. Serve as appetizers.

9 min.   hot   none

Father's Fourth of July Grilled Salmon

1 cup Backyard Lemon Butter Seasoning (see below)
2 cups Italian dressing
1 whole 4- to 5-pound salmon
1/2 cup olive oil

---

*A blend of hickory and apple woods
will lend great flavor to this dish.*

In a large bowl, mix lemon butter and Italian dressing. Allow to stand for about 15 minutes. Take the salmon, fresh from the market, and rub it with olive oil, inside and out. Generously spread lemon butter mixture on the salmon, inside and out.

Place the salmon on heavy-duty aluminum foil or a well-greased grill rack. Cover the grill and cook over moderately high heat for about 10 minutes per pound, or until the fish flakes easily when tested with a fork. Leave the skin on for cooking, and peel back for serving. Cover with more lemon butter sauce as a garnish.

Backyard Lemon Butter Seasoning

Combine 1/4 cup lemon juice, 1/4 cup melted butter, 1 teaspoon ground dill, and 1 teaspoon garlic salt. Mix a large batch and use as needed with your favorite backyard recipes.

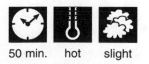

50 min.   hot   slight

9

Bob E.'s Smoked Stuffed Artichokes

4 large artichokes
2 tablespoons butter or margarine
4 tablespoons olive oil
1/4 cup chopped onion
1/4 cup chopped celery
1/2 cup chopped zucchini
1 clove garlic, pressed
1/4 cup lemon juice
1/4 cup shredded mozzarella cheese
1 teaspoon ground pepper
1 teaspoon salt
1/4 cup bread crumbs

Cook the artichokes in boiling salted water for 30 minutes. Remove and drain. Remove leaves and scrape out the fuzzy choke. Place the artichoke hearts, onion, celery, zucchini, and garlic in a saucepan with olive oil and butter. Simmer until the mixture is softened. Place the mixture in a food processor and purée. Combine with remaining ingredients, stir, and stuff into artichoke shells. Smoke over apple-wood fire for about 30 minutes.

30 min.   med.   slight

Rick's Hot Wings

5 pounds chicken wings
1/2 cup white vinegar
1/2 cup Backyard BBQ & Grill Seasoning (page 5)
1 pound butter or margarine
1 tablespoon Tabasco
1/4 cup Louisiana hot sauce

Prepare a wood or charcoal fire or preheat a gas grill.

Rinse the wings and pat dry. Place them in a clean trash bag. Pour vinegar over the wings, hold the bag tightly closed, and shake. Pour BBQ & Grill Seasoning in the bag and shake again. Arrange the wings on the grill and smoke for about 20 minutes. In a saucepan, melt the butter and add the Tabasco and hot sauce. Stir well, then brush half the mixture over the wings. Cook for another 5 to 10 minutes. Place the wings on a large platter, pour the remainder of the sauce mixture over, and serve.

35 min.   hot   light

Spicy Smoked Potato Skins

4 large freshly baked potatoes
1 stick (1/2 cup) butter or margarine, at room temperature
1/2 cup sour cream
1 teaspoon garlic powder
1 teaspoon chili powder
1 teaspoon ground black pepper
1 teaspoon salt
1 cup grated Cheddar cheese

Prepare a smoker or charcoal grill following the directions on page xxv, or preheat one side of a gas grill.

Slice the baked potatoes in half lengthwise. Spoon the pulp into a mixing bowl, leaving about 1/4 inch of potato on the skin. Add the butter, sour cream, and spices to the potato pulp and mix well. Stir in half the grated cheese.

Place the skins on aluminum foil or on a grill rack, and smoke over medium heat for about 30 minutes. Remove from the grill and fill each skin with potato mixture. Top with the remaining grated cheese and return to smoke for an additional 30 minutes, or until cheese is melted. Cut into bite-size pieces and serve hot.

1 hr.   med.   slight

Lemon Grilled Veggies

1 pound broccoli
1/2 pound cauliflower
1/2 pound potatoes
1/2 pound carrots
2 cloves garlic, pressed
1 cup olive oil
1 teaspoon salt
2 teaspoons pepper
1 large lemon
1 tablespoon lemon juice

Prepare a wood or charcoal fire or preheat a gas grill (medium heat).

Cut the broccoli and cauliflower into spears. Slice the potatoes into wedges and the carrots into thick strips. Mix the garlic, oil, salt and pepper and allow to stand for 15 minutes.

Boil the veggies in a large pot for about 3 minutes. Drain. Place on the grill rack away from the fire and baste with the oil mixture. Slice the lemon into thick rounds and add to the grill rack. Pour lemon juice over everything.

Grill, turning and basting occasionally, until the potatoes are brown and the other vegetables tender, about 1 hour.

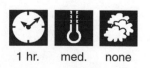

1 hr.   med.   none

Punctual
Perfection

1ST DEGREE
SPECIALTIES

Absolute Grilled Shrimp

1 1/2 pounds large shrimp
8 tablespoons (1 stick) butter
1/2 teaspoon garlic powder
1 tablespoon paprika
1/2 teaspoon celery salt
1/2 teaspoon dry mustard
1 tablespoon sugar
1/2 teaspoon ground sage
1/2 teaspoon onion salt

Make a wood or charcoal fire or preheat a gas grill (hot).

Prepare the shrimp: Shell and devein, leaving the tails on. Melt the butter and stir in the seasonings. Place the shrimp in a flat dish and cover with the herbed butter.

Refrigerate for 1 hour. Thread the shrimp on metal or well-soaked bamboo skewers or place on a grill rack. Grill for 3 to 4 minutes. Turn and grill for another 3 minutes. Baste the shrimp with the butter while cooking.

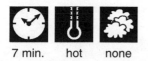

7 min. hot none

Grilled Haddock

4 haddock steaks, 1 1/4 inches thick
1/2 teaspoon salt
1/2 teaspoon pepper
1/2 cup flour
1/3 cup butter or margarine, melted

Prepare a wood or charcoal fire or preheat a gas grill to medium.

Sprinkle the steaks with salt and pepper, then dust with flour. Brush with melted butter. Place the fish on the grill rack and cook over a medium fire for 8 minutes. Brush with butter while cooking. The fish will flake when poked with fork when done, about another 4 minutes. Serve with fresh lemon halves and melted butter.

12 min.   med.   slight

Barbequed Fajitas

1/2 cup soy sauce
1/8 cup Backyard BBQ & Grill Seasoning (page 5)
1/4 cup white vinegar
1/4 cup white wine
2 pounds flank steak or skirt steak
2 green bell peppers, cored and sliced into eighths
1 large onion, peeled and sliced 1/2 inch thick
2 red bell peppers, peeled and sliced into eighths
1/2 cup black olives
Flour tortillas

Prepare a wood or charcoal fire or heat a gas grill to medium heat.

Combine the soy sauce, BBQ seasoning, vinegar, and white wine in a disposable foil baking pan. Soak the steak in this marinade for about 15 minutes. Drain the meat and place on the oiled grill. Add the vegetables to the marinade and place the pan on a hot part of the grill to cook while the steak is cooking. Meanwhile, wrap a stack of flour tortillas in foil and place them on a cool part of the grill.

Grill the steak for 7 to 8 minutes on each side. Slice thin and serve with the drained vegetables, to be rolled or folded into the tortillas.

16 min.   med.   slight

Grilled Polynesian Red Snapper

1 onion, minced
6 scallions, chopped
2 teaspoons thyme
2 teaspoons salt
1 teaspoon allspice
1/4 teaspoon grated nutmeg
1/4 teaspoon ground cinnamon
1/4 teaspoon ground red pepper
1/4 teaspoon ground black pepper
2 cloves garlic, minced
1/2 cup olive oil
1/4 cup soy sauce
2 red snappers, 2 pounds each, heads on and trimmed
1/3 cup fresh lemon juice
Grated zest of 1 lemon

This quick dish should serve 4 to 6 people. Serve on a bed of steamed rice with a pineapple garnish.

Combine the onion, scallions, thyme, salt, allspice, nutmeg, cinnamon, and peppers in a small bowl. Add the garlic, olive oil, and soy sauce. Mix until well blended. Clean the fish and coat with lemon juice inside and out. Brush with the sauce mixture.

Place the fish on a well-oiled hot gas grill and sprinkle with the lemon zest. Baste liberally with the remaining sauce while cooking about 8 to 10 minutes per side.

20 min.   hot   slight

Grilled Salmon Roberto

1/2 cup olive oil
2 teaspoons thyme
2 teaspoons salt
1 teaspoon garlic powder
1/4 teaspoon ground black pepper
1/4 teaspoon ground red pepper
1 onion, chopped
2 salmon steaks, 2 inches thick

Coat the salmon with olive oil and place in a clean glass dish; set aside. Mix the dry spices in a small bowl or mortar and pestle, then add the onion. Rub the spice mixture into each side of the salmon steaks, return to the dish, and refrigerate for 1 hour.

Cook on a hot gas grill for about 10 minutes on each side. The fish may be placed on the grill rack, on foil, or in a wire basket. Be sure to coat the surface that touches salmon with olive oil to prevent sticking.

20 min.   hot   slight

Easy Ed's Grilled Lobster Tails

1 stick butter or margarine
1/2 cup lime juice
1/2 cup lemon juice
1/4 cup minced onion
1 teaspoon thyme
1 teaspoon salt
1/4 teaspoon allspice
1/4 teaspoon grated nutmeg
1/4 teaspoon ground ginger
1/4 teaspoon ground black pepper
1/4 teaspoon ground red pepper
4 large frozen rock lobster tails, 8 ounces each, thawed

Melt the butter in a small saucepan and combine with the lime and lemon juice, onion, and spices. Rinse the lobster tails in cold water and split open the shells to expose the lobster meat, leaving it attached to the tail section. Coat the tails with the butter mixture and place on an oiled grill rack over a hot gas grill.

Cook for several minutes, turning frequently and basting with the butter mixture. Total cooking will be 8 to 10 minutes, or until the lobster becomes opaque throughout. Reserve a portion of the butter mixture to serve at table.

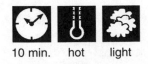

10 min.   hot   light

Kathy's Grilled Gulf Shrimp

8 tablespoons (1 stick) butter or margarine
1/2 cup lime juice
1/2 cup lemon juice
1/4 cup minced onion
1 teaspoon thyme
1 teaspoon salt
1/4 teaspoon allspice
1/4 teaspoon grated nutmeg
1/4 teaspoon ground ginger
1/4 teaspoon ground black pepper
1/4 teaspoon ground red pepper
2 to 3 pounds Gulf shrimp

Melt the butter in a small saucepan. Add the lime and lemon juice, onion, and all the spices. Shell and devein the shrimp and thread about 10 shrimp on each set of 2 metal skewers held close together and parallel to each other. Skewer about 1/4 inch from the head on one and about 1/4 inch from the tail on the other. This method will allow you to flip the shrimp without their plopping around. Brush with the butter mixture and place on a very hot gas grill. Continue to baste as flames shoot up from the grill. Use caution but turn frequently. The shrimp will be pink and the butter will slightly burn to a golden brown in spots when done. Total cooking time will be 8 to 10 minutes.

10 min.   hot   slight

Stacey's Honey & Garlic Grilled Shrimp

3 cloves garlic, pressed
1/4 cup lemon juice
1/2 cup honey
1 teaspoon ground red pepper, or to taste
1/2 teaspoon salt
2 pounds large shrimp
1 stick butter or margarine

Combine the garlic, lemon juice, honey, pepper, and salt in a small bowl. Stir until honey doesn't stick to the side of the bowl; add more lemon juice if needed.

Rinse and devein the shrimp, but leave the shells on. Place the shrimp on a baking sheet and cover with the sauce mixture. Refrigerate for at least 1 hour, turning the shrimp about every 15 minutes until well coated with sauce. Meanwhile, preheat a gas-fired grill.

Melt the butter in a small dish or saucepan. Place shrimp on an oiled grill rack over a hot grill. Drizzle melted butter over the shrimp until flames erupt. Allow the shrimp to broil for about 4 to 5 minutes; turn and allow to broil an additional 4 to 5 minutes. Should serve 4 people as a main course or a number of guests as a great party appetizer.

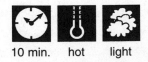

10 min.   hot   light

Tricky's Grilled Scallops

4 tablespoons (1/2 stick) butter or margarine
1/3 cup extra virgin olive oil
1 onion, minced
1 pound fresh scallops
1/3 cup California Chardonnay
2 teaspoons rosemary
2 teaspoons dried basil
1 teaspoon salt
1/4 teaspoon ground black pepper
1/4 teaspoon ground red pepper

The iron skillet on the grill is a great presentation touch while entertaining on the patio or deck.

Place a large iron skillet on your preheated gas grill. Heat the butter and oil in the pan until smooth. Stir in the onion and cook about 5 minutes, or until tender. Add the scallops and continue to cook until they change in color. Make sure to stay at the grill while cooking scallops as they can over-cook easily. Add the wine and spices as the color turns. Remove from the heat and serve at once.

10 min.   hot   slight

Ruffie's Wild Roughy

2 pounds orange roughy
1 lemon, sliced
1 orange, sliced
1/2 onion, peeled and sliced
4 tablespoons (1/2 stick) butter or margarine
1 teaspoon cracked black pepper
1 clove garlic, chopped
1/2 teaspoon salt

Pat the fish dry with paper towels and set aside. Preheat a gas-fired grill.

Make a bed of half the lemon, orange, and onion slices on a large piece of heavy-duty aluminum foil. Sprinkle with half the garlic, salt, and pepper. Place the fish in one layer on the bed and cover with remaining lemon, orange, and onion slices and the seasonings. Dot with the butter. Fold foil over the top and crimp all the edges, making a tightly sealed pouch.

Place the pouch over a hot grill and cook for about 8 minutes. Turn; poke a hole in the top of the foil with a fork to release steam. Cook for another 8 minutes or until the fish is cooked through.

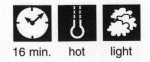

16 min.   hot   light

Schmidtly's Grilled Fish Medley

1 pound mahimahi
1 pound tuna fillet
1 pound salmon fillet
1 cup white zinfandel
1 teaspoon ground black pepper
1 teaspoon ground red pepper
8 tablespoons (1 stick) butter or margarine
1 onion, minced

With a sharp knife, cut the fish into bite-sized cubes 2 × 2 × 1-inch thick. Place in a large bowl and cover with the wine and pepper. Allow to marinate in the refrigerator for 30 minutes. Meanwhile, prepare a wood or charcoal fire or preheat a gas grill.

Melt the butter in a saucepan and add the onion. Sauté for about 5 minutes. Drain the fish and reserve the wine mixture in a small bowl. Place the fish on a well-greased grill rack on a hot grill. Drizzle with butter and onion. As flames shoot up, drizzle with the wine mixture. Continue cooking for about 8 to 10 minutes on each side or until done.

20 min.   hot   slight

Wendy's Spicy Gulf Shrimp

8 tablespoons (1 stick) butter or margarine
1/4 cup minced onion
1 cup olive oil
1 tablespoon Tabasco, or to taste
1/4 teaspoon ground black pepper
1/4 teaspoon ground red pepper
2 to 3 pounds Gulf shrimp

Melt the butter combined with the onion, olive oil, and seasonings in a small saucepan. Shell and devein the shrimp and place about 10 shrimp on each set of 2 skewers held close together and parallel to each other. Pierce the shrimp about 1/4 inch from the head on one skewer and about 1/4 inch from the tail on the other. This method will allow you to flip the shrimp easily. Brush with the butter mixture and place over a very hot gas grill. Continue to baste as flames shoot up from the grill. Use caution but turn frequently. The shrimp will be pink and the butter will slightly burn to golden brown in spots when done. Total cooking time will be 8 to 10 minutes.

10 min.   med.   slight

Great White
on the Grill

2 shark steaks
2 tablespoons butter or margarine
1 onion, peeled
2 lemons
1 tablespoon salt
1 tablespoon cracked black pepper

Prepare a wood or charcoal fire or preheat a gas grill. Tear off 2 sheets of aluminum foil, each large enough to enclose a steak completely. Grease the foil with the butter; place the steaks on the fire.

Slice the onion and lemons and place half on each piece of shark. Sprinkle with salt and pepper. Seal the foil tightly and place on the grill for about 10 minutes per inch of thickness, measured at the thickest point of the steaks. Remove from grill and let stand for 5 minutes. Carefully open the foil; the shark will be steaming. Place on a platter and serve hot.

10 min.   hot   slight

Spicy Grilled Trout

4 trout, heads removed
1/3 cup olive oil
1/3 cup wine vinegar
1 teaspoon garlic salt
1 teaspoon black pepper
1 teaspoon paprika
1 teaspoon ground red pepper
1 teaspoon dry mustard
1 teaspoon hot pepper flakes
1/4 cup water

Prepare a wood or charcoal fire or preheat a gas grill.

Clean the fish and pat dry. Mix the remaining ingredients in a small saucepan and bring to a boil. Rub the fish and the grill rack with oil. Place the fish on the rack over a hot fire and brush with the sauce mixture. Grill for about 15 minutes in all, turning once (carefully) and basting often.

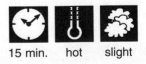

15 min.   hot   slight

Bob E.'s Chicken Steaks

4 boneless chicken breasts
4 tablespoons (1/2 stick) butter or margarine
1/2 teaspoon salt
2 tablespoons lemon juice
1/2 teaspoon marjoram
1/2 teaspoon paprika
2 lemons

Prepare a wood or charcoal fire or preheat a gas grill. Rinse the chicken breasts and pat dry.

Melt the butter and combine with the salt, lemon juice, and marjoram. Brush the chicken with the sauce and place on an oiled grill rack over hot coals. Grill 10 minutes, turn and grill for 5 to 6 minutes more. Sprinkle with paprika. Serve with fresh lemon halves.

16 min.   hot   slight

Kelsey's Grilled Catfish

4 catfish
1/2 cup red wine vinegar
1 tablespoon oregano
1 tablespoon salt
1 tablespoon coarse ground pepper
1/2 cup flour

Prepare a wood or charcoal fire or preheat a gas grill.

Clean and gut the catfish. Rub down with vinegar, inside and out. Combine the oregano, salt, pepper, and flour in a small bowl. Dust the cavity with the seasoned flour. Rub a little oil on the fish and place on an oiled grill away from direct heat, with the skin side down. Grill for 7 minutes. When the skin pulls back, grill for another 7 minutes. Cook for about a total of 15 minutes, using the indirect method.

15 min.   med.   light

Roughy in the Rough

3 pounds orange roughy
4 tablespoons butter or margarine
1/4 cup minced onion
1/4 cup minced parsley
1 teaspoon salt
1 teaspoon ground black pepper
4 strips lean bacon
4 lemon wedges

Prepare a charcoal fire. Wash the roughy and pat dry. Cut a 12-inch square of aluminum foil for each piece of roughy, and lightly butter each square. Place the roughy on the foil and sprinkle with onion, parsley, salt, and pepper. Place a whole or half strip of bacon on each piece of roughy and fold up the foil. Seal tightly. Set the foil packages directly on white hot coals. Cook for about 15 minutes, turning every 5 minutes. Serve with fresh lemon wedges.

15 min.   hot   slight

Randy's Bootz Steak

4 rib-eye steaks
2 cups red wine
2 tablespoons oregano
2 tablespoons salt
2 tablespoons coarse black pepper
1/2 cup raspberry preserves
1 cup barbeque sauce
1 teaspoon Tabasco

Marinate the steaks for about 2 hours in the wine mixed with the oregano, salt, and pepper. Prepare a charcoal fire or preheat a gas grill. Cook the steaks over a hot fire for about 7 minutes on each side. Mix the raspberry preserves and barbeque sauce. Add the Tabasco and pour over the steaks.

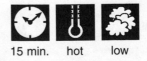

15 min.   hot   low

Grilled Polynesian Pork Steaks

1 onion, minced
2 teaspoons thyme
2 teaspoons salt
1/4 teaspoon ground black pepper
1/4 teaspoon ground red pepper
2 cloves garlic, minced
1/2 cup olive oil
1/4 cup soy sauce
6 pork steaks, 1 inch thick
1/3 cup fresh lemon juice
Zest of 1 lemon

Preheat a gas grill. Combine the onion, thyme, salt, and peppers in a small bowl. Add the garlic, olive oil, and soy sauce; whisk until thoroughly blended. Wipe the steaks with paper towel and coat with lemon juice. Brush each side of the steaks with the sauce.

Sear the steaks over high heat and sprinkle with the lemon zest. Remove to the cool side of the grill and close the lid. Baste liberally with the remaining sauce while cooking about 10 minutes per side or until the steaks reach an internal temperature of 170 degrees.

25 min.   hot   none

Grilled Baby Back Ribs

1/4 cup white vinegar
1/2 cup olive oil
3 cloves garlic, pressed
2 slabs baby back pork ribs
2 teaspoons salt
1 teaspoon cayenne pepper
1/4 teaspoon ground black pepper
1/4 teaspoon ground sweet red pepper

The secret to great pork ribs is to remove the thin membrane from the back side of the ribs. After removal, rub the ribs with white vinegar, then with olive oil. Continue to rub the ribs with the remaining seasonings, then let stand for about an hour.

Preheat a gas grill. Place two handfuls of dry hickory chips on the lava rocks on the hot side of the grill and a large foil or metal pan of water on the grill rack, directly over the fire. Arrange the ribs on the cold side of the grill and close the lid.

The cooking process should take about an hour over medium heat. Every 15 minutes, sprinkle the remaining baste mixture on the ribs. Cook until the internal temperature (away from bones) reaches 170 degrees.

1 hr.   med.   slight

Kev the Rev's Grilled Pork Tenderloin Supreme

2 small pork tenderloins
1 cup white vinegar
1/2 cup fat-free Italian dressing
1 onion, minced
1 teaspoon garlic powder
1 teaspoon salt
1 teaspoon ground black pepper
1 teaspoon ground red pepper
1 teaspoon paprika

Rub the meat with vinegar, then with the Italian dressing. Continue to rub the remaining seasonings into the loins and let stand for about half an hour in the refrigerator. Meanwhile, preheat a gas grill.

Place two or three handfuls of damp hickory chips on the lava rocks on the hot side of the grill and a large foil or tin pan of water on top of the lava rocks, directly over the fire. Sear the loins over the hot side of the grill, about 2 or 3 minutes on each side, then move to the cold side of the grill and close the lid.

The cooking process should take about an hour on high heat. Keep the loins close to each other to help retain moisture. Every 15 minutes sprinkle the remaining baste mixture on the loins. Cook until the internal temperature reaches 170 degrees.

1 hr.   high   light

Grilled Lemon & Orange Monkfish

2 lemons, sliced
2 oranges, sliced
1 onion, sliced
1 cup white wine
1 clove garlic
1/4 teaspoon salt
1 teaspoon ground black pepper
4 pounds monkfish fillets

Lay the fruit and onion slices in a rectangular baking dish. Cover with a mixture of the wine, garlic, salt, and pepper and allow the flavors to blend for about 1 hour. After an hour, add the fish, turning to coat all sides, and place in the refrigerator for another hour. Turn the fish once or twice.

Prepare a wood or charcoal fire or preheat a gas grill. Oil the grill rack. Grill the fish over a hot fire, searing on each side for about 1 minute. Cook on the indirect side of the grill 4 to 5 minutes on each side, or until flaky.

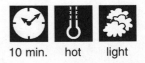

10 min.   hot   light

Bobby's Grilled Stuffed Pork Chops

2 cups croutons
1 cup orange juice
1 cup Italian dressing
4 tablespoons (1/2 stick) butter or margarine, melted
1/4 cup minced onion
1 tablespoon chopped parsley
1/4 cup chopped celery
1/4 teaspoon salt
1/2 teaspoon ground black pepper
1/2 teaspoon paprika
1/2 teaspoon ground red pepper
8 center-cut pork chops, 1 1/4 inches thick

Prepare a wood or charcoal fire or preheat a gas grill.

Soak the croutons in the orange juice in a large bowl. When soft, add the dressing, melted butter, onions, parsley, celery, and seasonings. Mix well. With a sharp knife, make a pocket in the pork chops along the fat side and in through the center of the meat. Fill each pocket loosely with stuffing. Close the openings with a wooden toothpick or bamboo skewer.

Sear the chops over a very hot fire for about 2 minutes on each side. Cook on the indirect side of the grill for about 20 minutes on each side or until the meat reaches 170 degrees, measured away from the bone and stuffing.

40 min.   hot   light

Freckles' Grilled Pork Shoulder

1 boned pork shoulder roast, 3 to 4 pounds
1 cup white wine
1 cup olive oil
3 cloves garlic, minced
1 onion, minced
1 teaspoon ground black pepper
1 teaspoon ground red pepper
Salt to taste

With a sharp knife, cut the pork into 1-inch-thick slices, against the grain. Marinate in a mixture of the wine, olive oil, and spices for about 1 hour.

Prepare a charcoal fire or preheat a gas grill. Grill the pork slices over a very hot fire like that for steaks. Sear each slice for 1 minute on each side. Transfer to the indirect side of the grill and cook about 20 minutes on each side, or until the internal temperature of each slice reaches 170 degrees.

As the pork cooks, pour the remaining marinade mixture on each slice to create steam in the grill unit.

40 min.   hot   slight

Wild Bill's BBQ Ribs on a Gas Grill

1 pound hickory and apple wood chips
1 quart apple juice
3 or 4 slabs pork spareribs, each weighing 2 1/2 pounds
    and down
1 cup white vinegar
1 tablespoon ground black pepper
1 tablespoon ground red pepper
1 cup olive oil
3 to 4 cloves garlic, pressed

Soak wood chips in the apple juice for about 30 minutes before cooking. Strip the membrane off the back side of the ribs and gently rub with vinegar. Allow to stand at room temperature for about 5 minutes. Mix the black and red pepper in a small bowl, then rub into the damp ribs. Rub each rib liberally with olive oil, then garlic.

Preheat one side of a gas grill. Stack the ribs on the indirect side, leaving the opposite side on medium to high heat. Place the damp wood chips on the hot side of the fire. Close the lid and allow the ribs to smoke, adding more wood chips every 45 minutes or when smoke dies down. The process should take about 3 hours, or until the rib meat reaches 170 degrees away from the bone. It is better to start with a lower fire and cook longer than to start too hot and dry out the ribs.

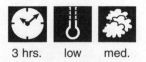

3 hrs.   low   med.

41

Rick's Grilled Pork Kebabs

1 boneless pork butt roast, 2 to 3 pounds
1 cup white vinegar
1 cup Italian dressing
1 tablespoon ground black pepper
1 tablespoon ground red pepper
12 cherry tomatoes
12 cocktail onions
12 chunks green bell pepper
12 chunks red bell pepper
12 small parboiled whole new potatoes
1 small bag hickory wood chips

Cut the meat into 2-inch chunks and marinate in a mixture of the vinegar, Italian dressing, and black and red pepper in the refrigerator for about 2 hours. Alternate chunks of meat and vegetables, on large metal skewers.

Prepare a wood or charcoal fire or preheat one side of a gas grill. Sear the kebabs over a hot fire for 1 minute on each side. Add a handful of wood chips to the hot side of the fire and close the lid. Cook the kebabs on the indirect side of the grill for about 35 minutes or until the pork reaches an internal temperature of 170 degrees and the vegetables are tender.

37 min.   hot   slight

Mac's Hot Buttered Swordfish

4 swordfish steaks, cut 1 inch thick
1 teaspoon salt
1 teaspoon ground black pepper
8 tablespoons (1 stick) butter or margarine
Juice of 2 lemons
2 tablespoons anchovy paste
1 clove garlic, minced
Paprika to taste
Red and white pepper to taste

Prepare a wood or charcoal fire or preheat a gas grill.

Sprinkle the swordfish on both sides with the salt and black pepper and place on a sheet of heavy-duty aluminum foil. Melt the butter in a saucepan and add the lemon juice mixed with the anchovy paste and garlic. Baste the swordfish generously with this mixture, place foil and fish on the grill rack, and grill for 10 to 15 minutes or until opaque. Turn at least once, and continue to baste with the butter mixture. Do not overcook. Remove from the grill and top with a generous sprinkling of paprika, and red and white pepper.

15 min.   hot   light

Greek BBQ Kebabs

2 pounds boneless lamb steak,
    trimmed of fat and cut
    into 1 1/2-inch cubes
1/4 cup olive oil
1/2 cup lemon juice
1 tablespoon salt
1 tablespoon cracked black pepper
1 tablespoon dried dill
12 (1-inch) cubes green bell pepper
12 small onions, peeled
12 cherry tomatoes

Marinate the lamb in a mixture of olive oil, lemon juice, salt, pepper, and dill. Let stand for 20 to 30 minutes. Meanwhile, prepare a charcoal fire or preheat a gas grill.

Parboil the vegetables for about 3 minutes. Thread lamb and vegetables alternately onto metal skewers and grill for 10 to 15 minutes. Turn frequently and baste with the marinade while grilling.

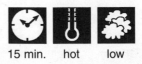

15 min.   hot   low

44

Wild Bill's Sizzlin' Sirloin

4 sirloin steaks, 12 ounces each
2 cups Big Bill's Favorite Steak Marinade (page 129)
1 tablespoon ground black pepper
1 teaspoon garlic powder

You can use your own favorite steak marinade, but try Big Bill's.
It's out of this world!

Marinate steaks for about 30 minutes while you prepare a charcoal fire or preheat a gas grill. Sear each side of the steaks over a hot fire for about 30 seconds. Move the steaks to the cool side of the grill, cover, and cook for 7 minutes. Flip, pour the remaining marinade over the steaks, and cook for another 7 minutes. This should produce the perfect medium-rare steak.

15 min.   hot   slight

Smoked Fish Steaks

1/2 cup soy sauce
2 tablespoons olive oil
1 clove garlic, chopped
1/4 cup chopped onion
1/4 teaspoon ground ginger
2 pounds fresh fish steaks, cut 1 1/2 inches thick

Combine the soy sauce, oil garlic, onion, and ginger. Set the marinade aside for 15 minutes for the flavors to blend. Place the fish in a large bowl and cover with the marinade. Allow to stand for 1 hour. Meanwhile, prepare a charcoal fire or preheat a gas grill. Soak some hickory chips in water for about 20 minutes; drain the chips and place directly on the fire.

Place the fish on a well-oiled grill rack and grill over medium heat for 15 to 20 minutes. Turn often and baste with the remaining marinade.

20 min.   med.   light

Too Cool T-Bones

2 T-bone steaks, cut 1 1/2 inches thick
2 tablespoons Italian dressing
8 tablespoons (1 stick) butter or margarine
1 cup sliced mushrooms
2 cloves garlic, minced
1 cup white wine
1 teaspoon salt
1 teaspoon cracked black pepper

Bring steaks to room temperature while you prepare a charcoal fire or preheat a gas grill. Brush the steaks with Italian dressing and sear on an oiled hot grill for 1 minute on each side. Move to the cool side of the grill, cover, and cook for 7 minutes. Flip, then cook for 6 minutes.

After searing and covering the grill, melt the butter in a small skillet and add the mushrooms and garlic. Sauté for 2 to 3 minutes; add the wine, salt, and pepper and simmer until the steaks are done. Pour the mushroom sauce over the steaks and serve.

14 min.   hot   slight

Grilled Minute Steak

1 cup flour
1 tablespoon ground black pepper
1 teaspoon ground red pepper
1 teaspoon paprika
1 tablespoon salt
2 eggs
2 pounds minute steaks

Mix the flour and seasonings in a large flat dish. Beat the eggs in another flat dish. Tenderize the steaks with a meat hammer. Beat very thin.

Dip the steaks in the egg bath, then in the seasoned flour. Generously coat both sides. Place on a well-greased hot gas grill and cook, flipping frequently, until the crust is golden brown. Serve with a spicy sweet barbecue sauce.

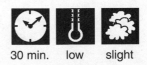

30 min.   low   slight

Ricky's Steak Flambé

1 sirloin steak, 2 inches thick
1 teaspoon salt
1 tablespoon ground black pepper
8 tablespoons (1 stick) butter, melted
1/4 cup Tanqueray gin

Bring the steak to room temperature. Prepare a wood or charcoal fire or preheat a gas grill.

Rub the steak with salt and pepper. Sear on each side on a well-oiled grill rack over a hot fire for about 1 minute. Move the steak to the cool side of the grill, cover, and cook for about 10 minutes. Turn and cook for about 7 minutes more.

Melt the butter in a saucepan, stir in the Tanqueray, and warm the mixture slowly. Place the steak on a warm metal serving tray. Ignite the butter sauce and pour over the steak. Present at table and slice while still flaming.

20 min.   hot   light

Ron & Dave's Mexican Jumping Steak

4 sirloin steaks, cut 1 inch thick
1 tablespoon ground cumin
1 tablespoon ground red pepper
1 tablespoon habañero pepper sauce
1 tablespoon Tabasco
1 tablespoon ground white pepper
1/4 cup water
1/4 cup white vinegar

Combine the spices with the water and vinegar. Marinate the steaks in the mixture for about 30 minutes, turning once or twice, while you prepare a charcoal fire or preheat a gas grill. Put the steaks on a hot well-oiled grill rack and cook to your liking—4 to 5 minutes on each side for rare. Brush marinade on the steaks while cooking.

10 min.   hot   slight

Mad Dog's Center-Cut Sirloin

2 center-cut sirloin steaks, cut 1 1/2 inches thick
1 cup hot water
2 tablespoons white vinegar
2 tablespoons No Misteaks Marinade (see below)
2 tablespoons No Misteaks Seasoning (see below)

Bring the steaks to room temperature. Combine the water, vinegar, and steak marinade. Mix well and let stand for 15 minutes, then pour marinade over the steaks and marinate for 15 minutes. Meanwhile, prepare a charcoal fire or preheat a gas grill.

Place the steaks on a hot well-oiled grill rack and sear for about 2 minutes on each side. Move the steaks to the cool side of the grill and brush with the marinade. Cover the grill and allow to cook for 7 minutes; flip and cook for 7 more minutes for a perfect medium-rare steak. Top with the steak seasoning and serve.

No Misteaks Marinade

Combine 1 part good-quality beef broth and 1 part Worcestershire sauce. Mix a large batch and use as needed with your favorite backyard recipes.

No Misteaks Seasoning

Combine 2 teaspoons garlic powder, 2 teaspoons onion powder, 4 teaspoons ground black pepper, and 2 teaspoons salt. Use as needed with your favorite backyard recipes.

18 min.   hot   light

Grilled Stuffed Flank Steak

1 flank steak, about 2 pounds
1 teaspoon salt
1 teaspoon ground black pepper
1/4 cup white wine
4 tablespoons (1/2 stick) butter or margarine
1 teaspoon dry mustard
1/2 cup minced mushrooms
1/2 cup minced onion
1 teaspoon garlic powder

Trim the steak to remove any fat. With a sharp knife, cut a deep horizontal pocket in the steak, but keep the opening as narrow as possible. Sprinkle some of the salt and pepper on the steak and set aside.

Prepare a charcoal fire or preheat a gas grill. In a skillet, combine the wine, butter, mustard, and remaining salt and pepper. Heat until the butter melts, then add the mushrooms and sauté for 2 minutes. Add the onion and garlic powder and stir. Pour off the excess liquid for use as a baste. Stuff the mushroom mixture into the steak and secure with small metal skewers. Grill over a hot fire for about 5 minutes on each side. Baste the steak after turning.

10 min. hot light

Absolute Lobster Tails

4 frozen rock lobster tails, thawed
8 tablespoons (1 stick) butter, melted
2 tablespoons dry white wine
1/2 teaspoon garlic powder
1 tablespoon paprika
1/2 teaspoon celery salt
1/2 teaspoon dry mustard
1 tablespoon sugar
1/2 teaspoon ground sage
1/2 teaspoon onion salt
Lemon wedges

Prepare a charcoal fire or preheat a gas grill.

Using a sharp knife, cut through and remove the top membrane of each lobster tail. Slightly loosen the meat from the shell. Combine the butter, wine, and spices in a small bowl. Stir well and brush over the lobster meat. Place the lobster tails, shell side down, on a grill rack or foil, away from the fire. Grill on low fire for about 30 minutes or until the meat is opaque. Serve immediately with lemon wedges and melted butter.

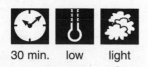

30 min.   low   light

George's Championship Sausage

2 pounds bulk Italian sausage
2 tablespoons dry rub
2 tablespoons onion flakes
2 tablespoons Worcestershire sauce
1 cup barbecue sauce

Combine all the ingredients in a mixing bowl, working the
spices in with the sausage. Use your favorite dry rub—
George's is a secret. (See the section on Sauces, Rubs, and
Marinades, pages 127–144.) Form the sausage into patties
and smoke over a hickory fire for about 30 minutes, following the instructions on smoked sausage technique, page
xxvii. Pour on your favorite barbecue sauce (George's is a
secret too!).

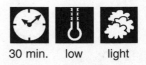

30 min.   low   light

The Kansas City Strip

4 Kansas City strip steaks, cut 1 inch thick
1/4 cup Worcestershire sauce
2 teaspoons salt
4 teaspoons ground black pepper
2 teaspoons garlic powder
4 tablespoons (1/2 stick) butter or margarine

Bring the steaks to room temperature while you prepare a charcoal fire or preheat a gas grill. Place the steaks on a flat dish and pour on Worcestershire sauce. Sprinkle on salt, pepper, and garlic. Allow to marinate for about 15 minutes. Sear the steaks for about 1 minute per side on a hot grill. Move the steaks to the cool side of the grill and cook covered for 7 minutes; flip and cook covered for 5 more minutes. Place a pat of butter on each steak. Leave steaks on the grill for 1 more minute and serve.

18 min.   hot   slight

Rick's Champion Rack of Lamb

6-rib rack of lamb
1 cup Italian dressing
1/2 cup Backyard Lemon Butter Seasoning (see below)
1 teaspoon salt
1 teaspoon cracked black pepper

Prepare a charcoal fire or preheat a gas grill. Combine the lemon butter seasoning and the Italian dressing. Allow to stand for 15 to 20 minutes. Salt and pepper the lamb and place on the indirect side of the grill for 15 minutes. Slice the rack into chops; top each medallion with some of the lemon butter mixture. Return to the grill for about 10 minutes, turning the chops once.

Backyard Lemon Butter Seasoning

Combine 1/4 cup lemon juice, 1/4 cup melted butter, 1 teaspoon ground dill, and 1 teaspoon garlic salt. Mix a large batch and use as needed with your favorite backyard recipes.

30 min.   med.   slight

Mad Dog's Pork Steaks

6 pork steaks, cut 1 inch thick
6 tablespoons white vinegar
6 tablespoons soy sauce
6 tablespoons Backyard BBQ
   & Grill Seasoning (page 5)

Prepare a charcoal fire or preheat a gas grill. Rub the steaks
with vinegar and soy sauce. Soak both sides, then sprinkle
with Backyard BBQ & Grill Seasoning. Grill for about 15
minutes on each side. For a slightly spicy taste, allow the
steaks to marinate for several hours before grilling.

30 min.   hot   slight

Margarita's Chicken

8 boneless chicken breast halves
1/2 cup olive oil
1/4 cup lemon juice
1 tablespoon dried dill
1 teaspoon ground cumin
1 teaspoon salt
1 teaspoon ground red pepper
8 tablespoons (1 stick) butter or margarine
1 clove garlic, pressed

Prepare a wood or charcoal fire or preheat a gas grill. Coat the chicken breasts with a mixture of the olive oil and lemon juice. Sprinkle with the dill, cumin, salt, and red pepper. Melt the butter and add the garlic. Pour garlic butter over the breasts and grill for 10 to 15 minutes per side over a hot fire.

30 min.   med.   slight

Grilled Beer Brats

8 bratwursts
2 bottles dark German beer
1 clove garlic, pressed

Prepare a charcoal or wood fire or preheat a gas grill.
  Place the brats in a disposable foil pan over a hot grill.
Add the beer and garlic and bring to a boil. Remove the
brats, split them lengthwise, and grill them over hot coals
about 3 minutes per side. Turn frequently.

8 min.   hot   slight

Cap'n Happy's Lemon Grilled Bass

1 whole bass, cleaned
1/4 cup lemon juice
4 tablespoons (1/2 stick) butter or margarine, melted
2 tablespoons chopped fresh dill
Salt and pepper to taste

Prepare a wood or charcoal fire or preheat a gas grill.

Split the bass in half and rub with lemon juice. Brush the fish on both sides with melted butter and sprinkle with salt and pepper. Place on a well-oiled grill rack, skin side down, and grill without turning for 10 minutes per inch of thickness, measured at the thickest point. Baste with a mixture of the remaining lemon juice, butter, and dill. Remove the skin after grilling.

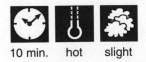

10 min.   hot   slight

Ricky's Porked Chops

4 pork chops, 1 1/2 inches thick
1 clove garlic, pressed
4 tablespoons (1/2 stick) butter or margarine
1/4 cup orange juice
1 onion, chopped
1 tablespoon dried marjoram
1 cup bread crumbs
1 teaspoon salt
1 teaspoon ground black pepper

Prepare a mesquite or charcoal fire or preheat a gas grill and add moistened mesquite chips. Trim the chops and cut a pocket into the side of each. Melt the butter and set aside. Combine the remaining ingredients in a mixing bowl, stir well, and stuff into the chops. Grill over mesquite fire for 30 minutes. Brush with butter and turn frequently.

30 min.   med.   light

Jay and David's Award-Winning Mustard Steak

2-pound center-cut sirloin steak
1/4 cup prepared yellow mustard
1/4 cup Worcestershire sauce
1 teaspoon cracked black pepper

Place the steak on a flat dish and bring to room temperature. Spoon mustard onto the steak and rub with your fingers. Add the Worcestershire sauce and continue to rub until both sides of the steak are covered with a tan mixture. Sprinkle generously with pepper. Allow to stand for about 30 minutes while you prepare a charcoal fire or preheat a gas grill.

Grill the steak on a well-oiled grill rack over high heat for about 8 minutes. Turn and continue cooking for another 7 minutes or until the meat reaches the desired degree of doneness.

15 min.   hot   light

Bidnessmen's Beef Burgers

2 pounds ground chuck
1/4 cup Worcestershire sauce
1 teaspoon garlic powder
1 tablespoon cracked black pepper
1/4 cup minced onion
1/4 cup minced green bell pepper
2 tablespoons Backyard BBQ & Grill Seasoning (page 5)
2 teaspoons No Misteaks Seasoning (page 51)

In a large bowl, combine the ground chuck, Worcestershire sauce, garlic, black pepper, minced onion, and green pepper. Mix thoroughly, then form into 8 equal balls. Flatten into patties, top with Backyard BBQ & Grill Seasoning and Steak Seasoning. Grill over a hot fire to your liking.

20 min.   hot   slight

Zesty Sir-Lime Burgers

2 pounds ground sirloin
1/4 cup lime juice
1 tablespoon sugar
1 tablespoon grated lime zest
1 clove garlic, pressed
1 egg

Combine all the ingredients in a bowl and mix well. Form into 6 to 8 patties and grill over a hot fire to your liking.

15 min.   hot   slight

Grilled Breast of Lamb

2 1/2-pound lamb breasts
1 large onion, chopped fine
2 cloves garlic, pressed
1/2 cup olive oil
1 cup red wine
1 tablespoon cracked black pepper
1 teaspoon salt
1 teaspoon dried rosemary
1 teaspoon dried thyme

Trim fat from the lamb and place the lamb on a flat dish. Combine the remaining ingredients in a small bowl, stir well, and pour over the lamb. Marinate in the refrigerator overnight.

Prepare an apple wood or charcoal fire or preheat a gas grill. Drain the lamb and place on an oiled rack over high heat. Grill over apple wood for about 20 minutes on each side, basting with the marinade. The lamb will be done when the edges start to get brown and crispy.

40 min.   hot   light

Tina's Châteaubriand

4-pound beef tenderloin roast
Sea salt
Cracked black pepper
1 bay leaf
2 onions, sliced
1 clove garlic, crushed
1/2 cup olive oil

Rub the châteaubriand with sea salt and cracked black pepper. Place the meat in a glass dish with the bay leaf, onions, and garlic. Cover with oil. Marinate in the refrigerator for 2 to 3 hours, turning every 45 minutes.

Prepare a wood or charcoal fire or preheat a gas grill. Drain the meat, place on an oiled grill rack, and sear over a hot fire for about 2 minutes on each side. Finish cooking over slow heat for about 25 minutes, or until the meat reaches the desired degree of doneness, turning once.

25 min.   slow   slight

Kansas City Steaks with Red Wine Sauce

1 1/2 cups red wine
1 cup beef stock
1 shallot, minced
1/8 teaspoon dried thyme
2 tablespoons butter or margarine
2 tablespoons flour
Salt and pepper
6 Kansas City strip steaks

In a saucepan, boil 3/4 cup of the red wine until reduced by half. Add the stock and sauté the minced shallot in the butter. When the shallot is almost translucent, add a pinch of thyme and the flour. Cook on low heat for about 10 minutes, stirring often. Add the remaining red wine to the stock mixture, stirring constantly. Cook slowly for 10 to 15 minutes. Add salt and pepper to taste. Set the sauce aside and keep warm.

Prepare a wood or charcoal fire or preheat a gas grill. Place the steaks on an oiled grill rack and sear over high heat for 1 minute on each side. Continue cooking over indirect heat for 6 minutes on one side; flip and cook 8 minutes on the other for medium rare. Drizzle a little sauce over the steaks during the final minutes of cooking. Serve with the remaining wine sauce.

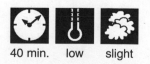

40 min.   low   slight

Mimi's Sweet and Sour T-Bones

1/2 teaspoon sesame oil
1/2 teaspoon canola oil
1/2 onion, minced
1 jalapeño pepper, chopped fine
1 ounce fresh gingerroot, chopped fine
Zest of 1 large orange
1/2 teaspoon thyme
1/2 teaspoon oregano
12 ounces orange juice concentrate
4 T-bone steaks

Preheat the oils in a saucepan, then add the onion, jalapeño pepper, ginger, orange zest, thyme, and oregano. Cover and cook over the lowest possible heat for 10 minutes. Add the orange juice and simmer uncovered for another 15 minutes.

Prepare a charcoal fire or preheat a gas grill. Place the steaks on an oiled grill rack and sear for 1 minute on each side. Continue cooking over indirect heat for 6 minutes on one side; flip and cook 8 minutes on the other for medium rare. Drizzle a little sauce over the steaks during the final minutes of cooking. Serve with remaining sweet and sour sauce.

30 min.   slow   light

The King's Club Filet Mignon

4 bacon-wrapped filet mignons
1/2 cup olive oil
1 teaspoon thyme
1/2 teaspoon salt
1 teaspoon garlic powder
1/4 teaspoon coarse ground black pepper
1/4 teaspoon ground red pepper
1 onion, chopped

Coat the filets with olive oil and place in a clean glass dish; set aside. Mix the dry spices in a small bowl or mortar and pestle, then add the onion. Rub the spice mixture into each side of the steaks, return to the dish, and refrigerate for 1 hour.

Preheat a gas grill. Place the filets on an oiled grill rack and sear over high heat for about 1 minute on each side. Cook over indirect heat for 6 minutes on one side, flip and cook 8 minutes on the other for medium rare. Drizzle with the remaining marinade mixture during the last minutes of cooking.

16 min.   hot   slight

Rick, Bill, & Bruce's Kansas City Grilled Rib-Eye

6 prime rib-eye steaks, cut 1 1/2 inch thick
8 tablespoons (1 stick) butter or margarine
1 cup extra virgin olive oil
1 large onion, minced
1 pound fresh mushrooms, sliced
1 cup Merlot or other full-bodied dry red wine
1/2 teaspoon dried rosemary
1 teaspoon dried basil
1/4 teaspoon salt
1/2 teaspoon ground black pepper
1/2 teaspoon ground red pepper

---

*The iron skillet on the grill is a great presentation touch
while entertaining on the patio or deck.*

Sear the steaks over a hot gas grill for about 1 minute on each side. Cook over indirect heat for 6 minutes on one side; flip and cook 8 minutes on the other side for medium rare.

Place a large iron skillet on your gas grill. When the steaks are about halfway done, heat the butter and oil in the pan until the butter melts. Stir in the onion and cook until tender. Add the mushrooms and continue to cook until they change in color. Make sure to stay at the grill while cooking the mushrooms, as they can overcook easily. Add the wine and spices as color turns. Remove from heat and serve at once.

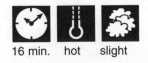

16 min.   hot   slight

70

Gwen's Grilled Stuffed Prime Rib Steak

2 cups croutons
1 cup orange juice
4 tablespoons (1/2 stick) butter or margarine, melted
1/4 cup minced onion
1 tablespoon chopped parsley
1/4 cup chopped celery
1/4 teaspoon salt
1/2 teaspoon paprika
1/2 teaspoon ground red pepper
1/2 teaspoon ground black pepper
1/2 cup fat-free Italian dressing
4 prime rib steaks, center cut, 1 1/4 inches thick

Soak the croutons in orange juice in a large bowl. When soft add melted butter, onions, parsley, celery, salt, and spices. Mix well. With a sharp knife make a deep horizontal pocket in each steak along the fat side and in through the center of the meat. Stuff each pocket with stuffing. Close the openings with a wooden toothpick or bamboo skewer.

Preheat a gas grill. Sprinkle the meat with additional salt and pepper to taste and sear over a very hot fire for about 2 minutes on each side. Continue cooking on the indirect side of the grill for about 8 minutes on each side or until the meat reaches 135 degrees.

20 min.   hot   light

Riley Dog's Lemon & Butter Breasts

8 chicken breast halves
1 cup fresh lemon juice
8 tablespoons (1 stick) butter or margarine
8 teaspoons lemon pepper

Place the breasts on a cookie sheet. Make a horizontal slit in the thickest part of each breast and stuff with 1 tablespoon of butter. Pour lemon juice over the chicken, coating both sides, then sprinkle with lemon pepper.

Prepare a hickory wood or charcoal fire or preheat a gas grill. Place the breasts on an oiled grill rack and grill over medium heat for 50 minutes to an hour. Baste with lemon juice every 20 minutes.

1 hr.   med.   slight

Barbie's Grilled Chick Chick

3 pounds chicken breasts
3/4 cup white wine
1/4 cup water
1 onion, chopped
1 teaspoon salt
Freshly ground black pepper to taste
1/2 cup flour
1 tablespoon paprika
1 tablespoon ground red pepper
1 tablespoon ground white pepper
8 tablespoons (1 stick) butter

Clean, skin, and bone the chicken. Cut into 1-inch cubes.
Combine the wine, water, onion, salt, and freshly ground
pepper in a saucepan. Simmer the chicken in the wine mixture for about 15 minutes.

Prepare a charcoal or hickory wood fire or preheat a gas
grill. Combine the flour and remaining dry ingredients, mix,
and set aside. Allow the chicken to cool in the saucepan.
Drain and roll the chicken in the flour mixture. Brush with
melted butter, place on a grill rack, and grill over a medium
hickory fire, turning occasionally and basting with the
remaining butter, until brown.

35 min.   med.   light

Bob E.'s Pork Kebabs

2 pounds boneless pork roast
1/4 cup orange juice
1/4 cup lemon juice
1/2 cup olive oil
1/3 teaspoon salt
1/2 teaspoon black pepper
1 clove garlic, minced
2 green bell peppers, cored
2 red bell peppers, cored
1 jar large cocktail onions, drained
1 pound cherry tomatoes

Prepare a wood or charcoal fire or preheat a gas grill.

Soak hickory wood chips in water while the grill is heating. Cut the pork into 1 1/2-inch cubes and thread on metal or wet bamboo skewers. Combine the juice, olive oil, salt, black pepper, and garlic in a small bowl and allow to stand for 15 minutes. Brush the mixture on the pork, place the kebabs on an oiled grill rack, and grill for about 5 minutes. Turn the skewers and brush with marinade frequently. Transfer to the cool side of the grill and smoke over hickory wood for about 1 hour, following the directions on page xxvii. Cut the green and red peppers into cubes and place on skewers, alternating with onions and tomatoes. Grill for 5 to 7 minutes.

1 hr.   slow   slight

Cheater's Ribs

2 slabs pork ribs
2 tablespoons dry rub (page 134)
2 cups water
1/2 cup rye or bourbon whiskey
1/2 cup white vinegar

Cut the slabs in half or in thirds so that they fit in a Crock-Pot. Sprinkle with dry rub and place in the Crock-Pot. Pour in the water, taking care not to wash the spice from the ribs. Do the same with the whiskey and vinegar. Place the lid on the Crock-Pot. Set it for low heat and go to work.

After you get home, light a charcoal grill and let the coals blaze until 80 percent ashed. Add a handful of dampened hickory chips to the charcoal. Place the ribs on the grill and smoke for about 1 hour (see directions on page xxvii). Your friends will think you spent the whole day at home smoking!

1 hr.   low   light

**Extended
Excellence**

2ND DEGREE
SPECIALTIES

Down & Dirty Ribs

4 large slabs, pork spareribs
1/4 cup Worcestershire sauce
1/2 cup firmly packed brown sugar
1/4 cup granulated sugar
1 cup red wine
2 tablespoons salt
1 tablespoon ground habañero or other very hot dried chili
    pepper
1 large onion, chopped

Combine all the ingredients in a large bowl. Marinate the ribs for about 1 hour while you prepare a hickory wood or charcoal fire. Smoke the ribs over medium heat for about 2 hours. Baste every half hour with the marinade.

2 hrs. medium slight

Kathleen's Ham

10-pound fully cooked ham
20-30 whole cloves
1 small can pineapple slices
1/2 cup firmly packed brown sugar

---

*Ham isn't really barbeque, but it's cheap for a backyard party.
And this recipe tastes pretty good.*

Drain the juice from the pineapple and mix the juice with
the brown sugar. Take a sharp knife and draw a grid, cutting
the fat in a large crisscross pattern 1/8 inch deep across the
ham. Place a clove in the center of each square. Place a cou-
ple of pineapple rings on top of the ham and pour the sugar
mixture over all. Smoke for about 2 hours at 225 degrees, following the guidelines on page xxvii.

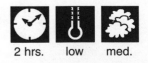

2 hrs.   low   med.

A-Dorr-Able Ribs

4 slabs St. Louis-cut ribs
1 can Budweiser beer
2 tablespoons paprika
2 tablespoons salt
2 tablespoons dry mustard
2 tablespoons ground black pepper
2 tablespoons ground white pepper
1/4 cup firmly packed brown sugar

Trim the ribs, removing feather bones. Brush the ribs with beer, then sprinkle with spices. Top with brown sugar, then seal two slabs each in aluminum foil. Bake the ribs in the oven at 225 degrees for about 2 hours. Remove from the oven, remove and discard the aluminum foil, and smoke the ribs over a hickory fire for about 2 hours. Baste with beer every 20 minutes.

2 hrs.   slow   slight

Kim's Teriyaki Grilled Chicken

1/2 cup soy sauce
1/4 cup firmly packed brown sugar
2 cloves garlic, pressed
2 tablespoons cracked black pepper
2 tablespoons olive oil
1 teaspoon ground ginger
4 large chicken breast halves

Combine the soy sauce, brown sugar, garlic, pepper, oil, and ginger in a large bowl and allow to stand for about 15 minutes for flavors to blend. Pour over the chicken and marinate for 2 hours.

Prepare a wood or charcoal fire. Place the breasts on a well-oiled grill and cook over low heat, turning and basting with the marinade, for about an hour. Remove from the heat, debone, and return to the grill for about another hour over a hickory fire.

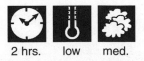

2 hrs. low med.

Baa Baa, Oink Oink Sausage

1 pound boneless pork butt
1 pound boneless lamb shoulder
2 cloves garlic, pressed
1/2 cup minced onion
1/4 cup lemon juice
2 tablespoons cracked black pepper
1 tablespoon salt
1/4 cup olive oil
1/4 cup white wine
6 feet sausage casings
2 cans beer

Prepare a wood or charcoal fire or preheat a gas grill. Run the pork and lamb through a meat grinder, then mix with the garlic, onion, lemon juice, pepper, salt, olive oil, and wine. Stuff into the casings. Pour 2 cans of your favorite beer in a large disposable foil pan over a hot charcoal fire. Place the sausages in the beer and bring the beer to a boil. Cook about an hour and a half. Remove with tongs and grill the sausages over a hot fire until brown, about 15 to 20 more minutes.

2 hrs.   hot   light

Smoked Tenderloin of Beef

6-pound beef tenderloin
1/2 cup olive oil
1/2 cup Italian dressing
2 garlic cloves, pressed
1 teaspoon ground rosemary
2 tablespoons cracked black pepper

Prepare a hickory fire in a smoker or charcoal grill. Rub the tenderloin with a mixture of the olive oil and the Italian dressing, then with a mixture of garlic, rosemary, and pepper. Place the tenderloin on an oiled rack and smoke over hickory for about 2 hours, or until the internal temperature reaches 150 degrees for medium rare. (See page xxvii for general directions.)

2 hrs.   slow   light

AB's Mutton

3 mutton chops, trimmed
1 cup white vinegar
1 tablespoon paprika
1 tablespoon dry mustard
1 tablespoon ground red pepper
1 tablespoon salt

Soak the chops in vinegar for about 15 minutes. Mix the spices in a small bowl. Sprinkle on both sides of chops. Smoke for about 2 hours over a hickory fire, following the directions on page xxvii.

2 hrs.   slow   slight

Smoked Lamb Shoulder

5-pound lamb shoulder roast
4 cloves garlic, pressed
1 teaspoon paprika
1 teaspoon dried rosemary
1/4 cup olive oil
1 teaspoon cracked black pepper
1 teaspoon salt

Remove the fat from the lamb and place the meat on a flat dish. Combine the garlic with the remaining ingredients in a medium-sized bowl. Mix well and rub into the lamb. Allow to marinate for about an hour. Smoke over hickory fire for about 2 hours (see the directions on page xxvii).

2 hrs.　　slow　　slight

Barbequed Burritos

2 pounds boneless pork butt
1 teaspoon salt
1 clove garlic, pressed
1/2 teaspoon ground cumin
1/2 teaspoon oregano, crushed
1 medium onion, sliced
Flour tortillas
1 cup guacamole
1 cup refried beans
1/2 cup salsa

Prepare a charcoal fire in a grill or smoker. Place the pork in a disposable foil pan and rub with salt, garlic, cumin, and oregano. Add 1 quart of water, or enough to come halfway up on the pork. Top the meat with the onion slices. Cook in a smoker with hickory wood for about 2 hours, or until the pork shreds with a fork. Keep water level at least halfway up on the pork.

For each burrito, heat a tortilla on the grill until hot but not dry. Place 1/2 cup of shredded meat on the tortilla and add 2 tablespoons of guacamole, 3 tablespoons of beans, and 1 tablespoon of salsa for each burrito. Roll up and serve immediately.

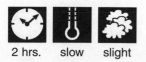

2 hrs.   slow   slight

Bob E.'s Boffo Burnt Ends

1 small flat beef brisket
1/4 cup white vinegar
1/4 cup soy sauce
1/4 cup dry rub (see page 134)
1/4 cup firmly packed brown sugar

Choose brisket about 12 inches long and 6 to 8 inches wide. Trim so that no fat is remaining on the meat. Rub with vinegar and soy sauce, then slice into five or six equal portions. When slicing, cut on the same angle as the small tip of the brisket. Try to make each piece look as if it is the end. Roll each piece in dry rub mixed with the brown sugar. Smoke for about two hours over a medium fire or until tips begin to burn. Remove from the smoker, cut into 1-inch cubes, top with your favorite barbecue sauce, and serve.

2 hrs.   med.   light

Smoked Salmon

1/3 cup olive oil
1/4 cup lemon juice
1/3 cup white wine
1 large onion, sliced
1 teaspoon salt
1 tablespoon ground black pepper
1 clove garlic, pressed
1 large whole salmon (7-10 pounds)
1/2 cup flour

Prepare a wood or charcoal fire. Combine the olive oil, lemon juice, wine, onion, salt, pepper, and garlic. Let stand for 15 to 20 minutes, then pour over the salmon. Allow the salmon to marinate for about 10 minutes in the refrigerator. Drain the fish and lightly dust with flour. Brush with more of the marinade.

Place the fish on a well-oiled grill rack or foil away from the fire and smoke for 1 1/2 hours, following the procedure on page xxvii. Brush with marinade while cooking. When the skin begins to stick and pulls away, smoke for another 30 minutes, for a total of about 2 hours.

2 hrs.   slow   slight

Dr. Daniels' Fiery Pork Steak

2 tablespoons ground red pepper
2 tablespoons paprika
2 tablespoons crushed red pepper flakes
2 tablespoons salt
2 tablespoons ground white pepper
1 tablespoon garlic powder
4 pork steaks, 2 inches thick
1 cup barbecue sauce

Prepare a wood or charcoal fire. Combine the spices and rub the seasoning into the steaks. Grill for about 7 minutes over high heat on each side. Move to the cool side of the grill, cover, and smoke for about an hour, brushing with barbecue sauce every 10 minutes.

75 min.   slow   slight

Country-Style Beef Ribs

1 tablespoon oregano
1 tablespoon ground white pepper
1 tablespoon garlic powder
1 tablespoon salt
4 to 8 pounds beef short ribs
1/4 cup olive oil
1/2 cup red wine vinegar

Prepare a wood or charcoal fire in a smoker or grill. Make a dry rub with the oregano, pepper, garlic powder, and salt. Rub the short ribs with oil and vinegar, then sprinkle with the rub. Place on a rack on the cool side of the grill and smoke over low, moist heat for 2 to 3 hours, following the directions on page xxvii.

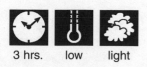

3 hrs.   low   light

Robbie's Ribs

4 slabs baby back beef ribs
2 tablespoons paprika
2 tablespoons ground black pepper
2 tablespoons salt
2 tablespoons sugar
2 cups Robbie's Rib Sauce (page 141)

Preheat the oven to 200 degrees. Remove the membrane from the ribs. Make a dry rub with the paprika, pepper, salt, and sugar. Rub generously on each slab. Tightly seal each slab in a piece of heavy-duty aluminum foil. Place the ribs on a cookie sheet and bake in oven for about two hours.

Prepare a hickory fire in a smoker or charcoal grill. Remove the ribs from the oven, discard the foil, and arrange the ribs on an oiled rack. Smoke ribs for about an hour and a half (see directions on page xxvii). Baste with Robbie's Rib Sauce every 30 minutes.

2 hrs.   slow   slight

Fritz's Flaming Pheasant

4 whole pheasants, thawed if frozen
1 cup lemon juice
1/4 cup sugar
1/2 cup white wine
1/2 cup Bacardi 151-proof Rum

Marinate the birds in a mixture of the lemon juice, sugar, wine, and half the rum for about 3 hours, turning several times.

Prepare a hickory fire in a smoker or grill. Place the birds on a well-oiled rack over low heat and smoke for about 3 hours, or until the internal temperature reaches 165 degrees. Place the birds on a serving tray. Heat the remaining 151-proof rum in a microwave until very warm. Pour over the birds and ignite. Present while flaming.

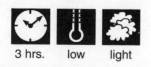

3 hrs.   low   light

Old Mill Gator

4 pounds fresh alligator steaks
1/2 cup vinegar
1 cup Old Mill BBQ Rib Rub
1/2 cup olive oil

Prepare a hickory fire in a smoker or charcoal grill. Brush the gator meat in vinegar and let stand for 15 minutes. Coat thoroughly with Old Mill BBQ Rib Rub. Seal in the spices by rubbing with olive oil.

Smoke the gator over a hickory fire for about 3 hours, following the smoking directions on page xxvii. If the gator begins to look dry, place it in a pan with a few tablespoons of water. Smoke until the water evaporates, another 30 minutes or so.

Old Mill BBQ Rib Rub

Combine 1/2 teaspoon garlic powder, 1/2 teaspoon onion powder, 1/4 cup Worcestershire sauce, 1 tablespoon anchovy paste, 1 tablespoon ground black pepper, 1 tablespoon paprika, 1 tablespoon sugar, 1 teaspoon ground red pepper, 2 tablespoons brown sugar, and 1 teaspoon salt.

3 hrs.   slow   med.

Spudly Beef Ribs

4 pounds beef short ribs, cut in 3-inch pieces
2 tablespoons ground black pepper
2 tablespoons salt
2 tablespoons sugar
4 pounds sliced russet potatoes
2 sticks (1/2 pound) butter or margarine
2 tablespoons yellow mustard

Rub the ribs with pepper, salt, and sugar. Smoke over a hickory fire for about 2 hours. Place the ribs and potatoes on a grill rack and cover with a butter and mustard mixture. Smoke until the potatoes are tender, about another hour.

3 hrs.   slow   slight

Ed's Beef Prime Rib Roast

4 to 5 pounds beef prime rib roast
2 teaspoons grated orange peel
2 cloves garlic, crushed
1 teaspoon sea salt
1 teaspoon cracked black pepper
1 teaspoon dried thyme leaves, crushed

Prepare a wood or a charcoal fire. Allow the meat to come to room temperature. Combine the orange peel, garlic, sea salt, black pepper, and thyme leaves. Rub the mixture evenly over the surface of the roast. Place the roast in a foil pan, fat side up, on a wire rack. Insert a meat thermometer into the thickest part of the roast, not touching either fat or bone.

Place the pan on the indirect side of the grill, leaving the alternate side on high. Wood chips may be added to the hot side of the grill for extra smoke flavor.

Cook on a hot grill (300 to 350 degrees) for 18 to 20 minutes per pound. A cooking thermometer should register 125 degrees for rare and 145 for medium. Remove the roast at the appropriate temperature, cover with a foil tent, and let stand for 15 to 20 minutes. The temperature will continue to rise by approximately 5 degrees. Trim excess fat before carving.

3 hrs.   med.   med.

Absolute Smoked Turkey

1 turkey, 10 to 15 pounds
1/3 cup olive oil
1/3 cup white wine
1/4 cup lemon juice
1 teaspoon ground black pepper
1 teaspoon salt
1 clove garlic, pressed
1/2 cup minced onion
1 teaspoon chopped parsley

Put the turkey into a deep container, such as a roasting pan. Combine all the remaining ingredients in a jar and shake until thickened. Brush the turkey with the marinade, inside and out, and set aside to marinate for 2 to 3 hours in the refrigerator. Pour off the marinade and smoke the turkey in a preheated grill, following directions on page xxvii, for about 3 hours. Use the indirect grilling technique with foil or grill rack.

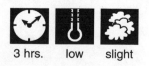

3 hrs.   low   slight

Dynamite Roast Beef

1 cup red wine
2 tablespoons cracked black pepper
2 teaspoons crushed red pepper flakes
1 teaspoon salt
1 tablespoon dry mustard
4-5 pound rump roast

Combine the wine, black and red pepper, salt, and mustard in a large bowl. Marinate the roast for about 30 minutes in this mixture while you prepare a wood or charcoal fire. Smoke the meat over a low hickory and mesquite fire about 2 hours, or until the internal temperature reaches 160 degrees for medium. Baste with the marinade while cooking.

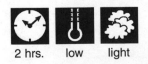

2 hrs.   low   light

Tough to Beat Burnt Ends

5-pound brisket
1 cup Italian dressing
1 tablespoon oregano
1/2 cup white wine
1/2 cup olive oil

Burnt ends are traditionally the last part of the brisket, cubed or pulled, and served with your favorite sauce. The main feature is a heavy layer of charring, plus the pink ring or smoke on the meat. The more sauce, the better.

Place the brisket and all other ingredients in a large zip-lock bag. Shake well and marinate in the refrigerator overnight. Smoke over a hickory fire for about 2 hours. Split into three equal sections and smoke for 2 more hours.

4 hrs.   slow   slight

Dijon Beef with Grilled Vegetables

1/4 cup Dijon mustard
1 cup red wine vinegar
1 1/2 teaspoons salt
1 tablespoon ground black pepper
1 clove garlic, pressed
1 top round beef roast, 2 to 4 pounds
2 cups broccoli florets
2 cups sliced carrots
2 cups cubed new potatoes
2 green bell peppers, chopped coarse
1 cup olive oil
1 cup Italian dressing

Combine the mustard, vinegar, salt, pepper, and garlic.
Spread on the meat and marinate for about 1 hour while you
preheat a smoker or prepare a charcoal fire. Coat the vegetables
generously with a mixture of olive oil and Italian dressing.

Smoke the meat until the internal temperature reaches
150 degrees. Add the vegetables to the smoker on a grill
rack. Cook everything until the meat reaches 160 degrees.

3 hrs.   med.   light

Red Wine & Dijon Chicken

1 cup red wine
1/2 cup Dijon mustard
1 tablespoon salt
2 tablespoons cracked black pepper
1 whole chicken, cut up

Mix the wine, mustard, salt, and pepper. Spread over the chicken parts and smoke over a low hickory fire for 3 to 4 hours. Brush with marinade every hour.

4 hrs.   low   slight

Mad Dog's Ribs

6 slabs spareribs, 2 1/2 pounds and down
1 cup Rick's Rib Rub
2 cups white vinegar
6 tablespoons olive oil
1 quart water

Trim and peel the membrane from the ribs. Rub generously with vinegar, sprinkle lightly with Rick's Rib Rub, then pour 1 tablespoon of olive oil on each slab. Rub well. Combine the remaining Rick's Rib Rub with the remaining vinegar and water to form a baste. Smoke the ribs over a hickory fire for 4 hours. Add hickory chips as needed and baste every 30 minutes.

Rick's Rib Rub

Combine 1 teaspoon paprika, 1/2 teaspoon ground red pepper, 1/2 teaspoon ground black pepper, 1 teaspoon salt, 2 teaspoons sugar, and 2 tablespoons brown sugar.

4 hrs.   med.   med.

Sharky's Ribs

4 slabs baby back ribs
2 cups white vinegar
2 tablespoons paprika
2 tablespoons ground red pepper
2 tablespoons ground black pepper
2 tablespoons salt
2 tablespoons brown sugar
2 tablespoons granulated sugar
2 tablespoons garlic powder
2 tablespoons onion powder
2 cups water

Remove the membrane from the back of the ribs. Sprinkle
ribs with 1 cup of vinegar and rub well. Make a dry rub
with all of the spices. Mix well. Use half the mixture to rub
onto both sides of the ribs. Place the ribs over a hickory fire
for 4 to 6 hours at 225 degrees. Meanwhile, combine the
water, 1 cup of vinegar, and the remaining dry rub and
shake well in a bottle. Baste the ribs with the mixture
every hour.

6 hrs.   slow   light

Bone's World Tour Honey Ribs

4 slabs baby back ribs
1 cup white vinegar
1/4 cup paprika
1/4 cup ground red pepper
1/4 cup salt
2 tablespoons ground black pepper
2 tablespoons sugar
1 cup clover honey

Peel the membrane from the back of the ribs. Rub the ribs generously with vinegar. Make a rub with the spices and sugar and generously rub into both sides of the ribs. Stack the ribs on top of each other and smoke slowly over a hickory fire for about 6 hours. Sprinkle with the remaining vinegar and rotate every hour. During the last hour, drizzle honey on each slab.

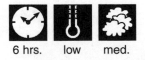

6 hrs.   low   med.

Lengthy
Leisure

3RD DEGREE
SPECIALTIES

R&B Tag-Team Pork Tenderloin

2 pounds pork tenderloin
1/4 cup olive oil
1/4 cup white vinegar
1 teaspoon paprika
1 teaspoon ground white pepper
1 teaspoon ground black pepper
1 teaspoon salt
1/4 cup Italian dressing
2 tablespoons Backyard Lemon Butter Seasoning (page 59)

Rub the tenderloin with olive oil and vinegar. Make a dry rub with the paprika, peppers, and salt, and rub into the pork. Smoke for about 1 hour with hickory and peach wood. Combine the Italian dressing and lemon butter. Spread over the meat after the first hour of smoking, then smoke for another hour or until the internal temperature reaches 160 degrees.

2 hrs.   slow   light

Mandarin Orange & Lemon Chicken

1/2 cup mandarin orange sections, puréed
1/2 cup lemon juice
1 clove garlic, pressed
1 teaspoon salt
1 teaspoon ground white pepper
4 large chicken breasts

Mix the oranges, lemon juice, and garlic. Sprinkle the salt and pepper on the chicken, then spread with orange sauce. Allow to marinate for 2 hours. Smoke over an apple and cherry wood fire for 2 to 3 hours or until the internal temperature reaches 160 degrees. Make sure to prop up the breasts with their bones, using indirect cooking method, (see page xix).

3 hrs.   slow   med.

Ralph's Prime Rib

1 standing rib beef roast, 4 to 6 ribs
1/4 cup olive oil
1/2 cup Worcestershire sauce
2 tablespoons beef broth
2 cloves garlic, crushed
2 tablespoons black pepper

Rub the roast with olive oil, then with Worcestershire sauce, and finally with beef broth. Crush the garlic and pepper together and rub into the roast. Allow it to stand in the seasoning mixture at room temperature for 2 hours, turning often. Drain and save the mixture for basting on the grill.

Place the roast on a preheated charcoal grill over indirect heat for 3 to 4 hours, or until the temperature reaches 125 degrees on a meat thermometer for rare meat, 140 degrees for medium rare. Baste every hour.

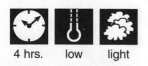

4 hrs.   low   light

City Market Special Leg of Lamb

1 whole leg of lamb
4 cloves garlic
1 cup olive oil
2 tablespoons cracked black pepper

Trim fat from the leg. Peel the garlic and cut into small pieces. Cut 1-inch-deep holes in the leg and stuff garlic into the holes. The leg should be well covered with holes and garlic. Rub with olive oil and sprinkle with pepper. Smoke over apple and hickory fire for three to four hours or until the internal temperature reaches 160 degrees in the thickest part of the leg. Serve with a mint sauce.

4 hrs.   slow   heavy

Wild Bill's Pork Tenderloin

2 pounds pork tenderloin
1 cup white vinegar
1 cup white wine
1 cup olive oil
2 tablespoons salt
2 tablespoons crushed red pepper flakes
1/4 cup Worcestershire sauce

Soak the loin in vinegar for about 30 minutes. Add the wine and olive oil and marinate for another 30 minutes. Drain and roll in salt and crushed red pepper. Smoke over a low hickory fire for about 3 hours. Baste with Worcestershire sauce every 30 minutes.

3 hrs.   slow   med.

Two-Dollar-a-Pound "Prime Rib"

1 (10 to 12-pound) top sirloin butt
5 ounces No Misteaks Marinade (page 51)
1/2 cup white vinegar
1 cup hot water
1/4 cup No Misteaks Seasoning (page 51)

A whole top sirloin butt (also known as boneless sirloin or rump roast) can be bought for about $2 per pound at most wholesale-club stores.

Bring the sirloin to room temperature. Mix the steak marinade, vinegar, and water, and allow to stand for about 5 minutes. Place the meat in a large mixing bowl and pour the mixture over. Allow to marinate for about 1 hour. Smoke over a hickory fire until the internal temperature of the sirloin reaches 125 degrees for very rare, 135 for medium rare, or 150 for medium. Sprinkle seasoning on the fire while cooking and at the table when serving.

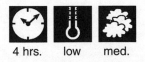

4 hrs.   low   med.

Sharky's Turkey Breast

1 (4-pound) boneless turkey breast
1 cup white vinegar
2 tablespoons paprika
2 tablespoons salt
2 tablespoons ground red pepper
2 tablespoons garlic powder
2 tablespoons olive oil

Rub the turkey with the vinegar, then sprinkle with the dry spices. Be sure to rub the spices into all surfaces and under the skin. Seal the spices in by rubbing with olive oil. Smoke for 4 to 6 hours, or until the internal temperature reaches 170 degrees.

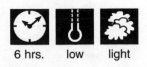

6 hrs.   low   light

George's Smoked Turkey Breast

2 large turkey breasts
1 cup white vinegar
1 cup olive oil
1/4 cup seasoning salt
3 tablespoons ground black pepper
3 tablespoons paprika
2 tablespoons garlic powder
3 tablespoons chili powder

Rub the breasts inside and out with vinegar; let stand for 15 minutes. Repeat the process with olive oil and let stand for 15 minutes. Make a dry rub with the seasoning salt, pepper, paprika, garlic powder, and chili powder. Rub breasts inside and out; refrigerate overnight. Smoke over a fruitwood fire for five to six hours, or until the internal temperature reaches 170 degrees.

6 hrs.   low   med.

George's Smoked Pork Roast

1 pork shoulder or butt, about 5 pounds
2 cups white vinegar
1 cup sugar
1/4 cup seasoning salt
5 tablespoons ground black pepper
3 tablespoons chili powder
2 teaspoons ground allspice
3 tablespoons paprika
1 teaspoon dried marjoram
1 1/2 tablespoons garlic powder

Cover the pork with vinegar and let stand for 30 minutes.
Make a dry rub with the remaining ingredients; rub into the
pork and refrigerate overnight. Smoke over a hickory fire for
6 to 8 hours, or until the internal temperature reaches 170
degrees.

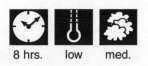

8 hrs.   low   med.

Andy's Jerked Deer

1 venison butt or shoulder roast, about 5 pounds
1 cup vinegar
1 cup Worcestershire sauce
1 cup Jamaican Jerk Spice (see below)

Marinate the venison in vinegar and Worcestershire for about 1 hour. Drain and rub generously with jerk spice. Smoke over a cherry wood fire for about 8 hours.

Jamaican Jerk Spice

If unavailable in your area, you can create your own mixture. For 1 cup of jerk spice, combine 1/2 cup ground allspice, 3 tablespoons paprika, 3 tablespoons ground red pepper, and 2 tablespoons ground white pepper. Better yet, see if you can get a prepared blend from a gourmet store.

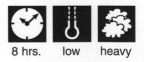

8 hrs.   low   heavy

Lemon & Garlic Leg of Lamb

1 leg of lamb, 5 to 6 pounds
1/4 cup olive oil
1/4 cup lemon juice
1 clove garlic, pressed
1 tablespoon ground black pepper
1/2 teaspoon salt

Remove excess fat from the lamb and place the leg in a large bowl. Combine the remaining ingredients in a small bowl and allow to stand at room temperature for about 10 minutes. Pour the mixture over the lamb and rub thoroughly. Cover with plastic wrap and marinate for 4 to 6 hours. Grill over hot coals for about 7 minutes on each side, then slow smoke over apple wood for about 8 hours.

8 hrs.   slow   med.

Sharky's Honey Mustard Ham

1 whole uncooked ham
2 cups Sharky's Mustard Sauce (see note below)
1/2 cup honey

Completely cover the ham with mustard sauce. Smoke over a hickory fire for about 6 hours. Pour the honey over the ham and slow smoke for 2 to 3 more hours.

Note: This fabulous creation can be found on page 143, or you can use your own mustard recipe. Try Sharky's recipe just once—it takes a bite out of anything you've ever had.

9 hrs.   slow   med.

Rick's Rib Rub Brisket

1 whole boneless fresh beef brisket, about 12 pounds
1 cup Worcestershire sauce
1/2 cup vinegar
1/4 cup No Misteaks Marinade (page 51)
1 cup Rick's Rib Rub (page 102)
1/4 cup No Misteaks Seasoning (page 51)

Trim the meat, leaving a quarter of an inch of fat on. Soak
the brisket in a mixture of Worcestershire sauce, vinegar, and
steak marinade for about 30 minutes. Rub with steak seasoning and rib rub. Smoke for about 10 hours at 250 degrees.

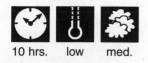

10 hrs.   low   med.

Sharky's Brisket

1 whole boneless fresh beef brisket, about 12 pounds
2 cups Worcestershire sauce
1 cup vinegar
2 tablespoons paprika
2 tablespoons salt
2 tablespoons ground red pepper
2 tablespoons beef broth
1/4 cup granulated sugar
2 tablespoons ground black pepper
2 tablespoons brown sugar

Trim excess fat from the meat. Combine all the other ingredients in a large bowl and let stand for about 30 minutes to let the flavors blend. Soak the brisket for about an hour in the mixture. Smoke the brisket over a hickory fire for 10 to 12 hours. Baste with the marinade every 2 hours.

12 hrs.   slow   heavy

GJD I & II—Foolproof Beef Brisket

1 (10-pound) boneless fresh beef brisket
1/4 cup lemon pepper
3 tablespoons MSG

Trim the brisket so that about 1/8 inch of fat remains. Remove the large knot of fat from the top of the brisket. Cover the brisket with lemon pepper and MSG. Slow smoke over a hickory fire for 10 to 12 hours.

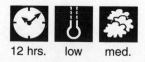

12 hrs.   low   med.

Honey & Garlic Smoked Brisket

1 (8-pound) boneless fresh beef brisket
4 cloves garlic, pressed
1/4 cup coarse black pepper
1 cup clover honey

Remove most of the fat from the brisket. Cover with pressed garlic and pepper. Place on the smoker, fat side up. Cover with honey and smoke over a hickory fire for 12 to 14 hours.

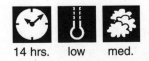

14 hrs.   low   med.

Pineapple Beach Brisket

1 (10-pound) boneless fresh beef brisket
1 cup crushed pineapple
1 cup firmly packed brown sugar
1 tablespoon paprika
1 tablespoon chili powder

Remove excess fat from the brisket, but leave some on for
flavor. Combine the pineapple, brown sugar, paprika, and
chili powder and spoon onto brisket. Smoke, pineapple side
up, for about 14 hours or until the internal temperature
reaches 160 degrees in the thickest part of the brisket.

14 hrs.   slow   med.

AB's Pseudo Brisket

1 (4-pound) boneless chuck roast
1/2 cup No Misteaks Marinade (page 51)
1/4 cup Worcestershire sauce
1/4 cup Rick's Generic Dry Rub (page 134)

Soak the roast for about an hour in the steak marinade and
Worcestershire sauce. Drain and save the liquid for basting.
Rub the roast with dry rub and smoke over a hickory fire for
about 16 hours. Baste every 2 hours with the marinade. Slice
very thin across grain, as you would a brisket.

16 hrs. slow heavy

Marathon Brisket

1/3 cup ground black pepper
1/3 cup firmly packed brown sugar
1/2 cup paprika
1/4 cup ground red pepper
1 whole fresh boneless beef brisket, about 14 pounds,
    untrimmed
1 cup olive oil

Combine the black pepper, brown sugar, paprika, and red
pepper in a large bowl and set aside. Rub the brisket with
olive oil, then with the spice mixture. Smoke over a slow
hickory fire for 10 hours. Remove from the smoker and
wrap in plastic film. Wrap again in aluminum foil. Return to
smoker for another 6 hours. Remove and let stand for several minutes before slicing thin.

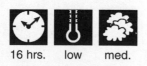

16 hrs.   low   med.

SAUCES, RUBS, AND MARINADES

Big Bill's Favorite Steak Marinade

1 1-ounce can BV Beef Broth
1/2 cup Worcestershire sauce
1/4 cup white vinegar
1 teaspoon garlic powder
1 tablespoon ground black pepper

Combine all the ingredients in a small bowl and allow to stand for 15 minutes. Pour half the mixture over steaks, turn the steaks, and cover with the remainder. Allow the steaks to marinate for 15 minutes before grilling. This batch is enough for four Kansas City strip steaks or two 1 1/2-inch center-cut sirloin steaks.

Black & Blue Rub

1 tablespoon black mustard seed
1 tablespoon cracked black pepper
1 tablespoon ground red pepper
1 tablespoon kosher salt
1 1/2 teaspoons dry mustard
1 1/2 teaspoons ground ginger
1/2 teaspoon ground black pepper
1/2 teaspoon ground white pepper
1/2 cup firmly packed brown sugar
1/4 cup granulated sugar

Combine all the ingredients and grind into a powder. For use as an interesting alternative to ordinary rubs.

Grapefruit & Honey Marinade

1/4 cup grapefruit juice
1 tablespoon grated grapefruit peel
1 teaspoon ground sweet red pepper
1/2 teaspoon cayenne
1/4 cup honey
2 tablespoons olive oil

Combine all the ingredients in a bowl and stir until well blended. Great for use on poultry or pork.

Mad Dog's Rib Rub

1/4 cup paprika
1/4 cup ground sweet red pepper
1/4 cup ground black pepper
1/4 cup granulated sugar
1/4 cup firmly packed brown sugar
1 tablespoon garlic powder
1 tablespoon ground white pepper
1 tablespoon cayenne pepper

Combine all the ingredients in a covered bowl and mix well. Use about 2 tablespoons of rub for each side of a rib slab. Rub the slab generously with white vinegar before adding rub. It kicks in the rub.

Orange & Cranberry Marinade

1 cup fresh cranberries
2 tablespoons honey
1 cup water
2 teaspoons grated orange zest
2 tablespoons fresh orange juice
1/2 cup white zinfandel
1/2 teaspoon salt
1 teaspoon ground black pepper

In a saucepan, combine the cranberries, honey, and water. Bring to a boil and simmer until the cranberries are soft. Strain the mixture through a sieve or fruit press, reserving the pulp and juice for the marinade. Add the remaining ingredients to the cranberry pulp and simmer over low heat for about 5 minutes. Chill until needed. One batch is enough for 2 large whole chicken breasts.

Rick's Generic Dry Rub

1/4 cup paprika
1/4 cup ground black pepper
1/4 cup salt

Use this rub as a base and add your favorite dry spices
to make your smoker the best on the block.

Combine these ingredients in a small bowl and mix well.
This rub can be used on any barbequed item. Just sprinkle
lightly on the intended food and rub. For a spicy taste,
sprinkle more heavily. This batch will do about 6 to 8 slabs
of pork ribs.

Sweet & Sour BBQ Marinade

1 cinnamon stick
1 teaspoon gingerroot minced fresh
1/2 teaspoon whole cloves
1/2 teaspoon mustard seed
1/2 teaspoon cayenne pepper
1 teaspoon whole black peppercorns
2 tablespoons honey
2 tablespoons sherry
2 tablespoons tomato paste
1 clove garlic, pressed
2 tablespoons soy sauce

Grind ginger, cloves, mustard, red pepper, and black peppercorns with a mortar and pestle until thoroughly blended. Combine with remaining ingredients in a medium bowl. Stir until well blended. Use on ribs, pork, or chicken.

Boiling BBQ Sauce

1 cup distilled water
1/2 cup green chili sauce
1/2 cup red chili sauce
1/2 cup A.1. steak sauce
1/2 cup white vinegar
1/2 cup firmly packed brown sugar
1 tablespoon chili powder
1 tablespoon celery seed
1 tablespoon salt
1 tablespoon ground black pepper
1 tablespoon habañero pepper sauce
1 tablespoon onion powder

Combine all the ingredients in a large saucepan. Bring to a boil; remove from heat. Use this sauce to bring your BBQ to life. It will "boil" long after it's been removed from the stove.

Kinda Karolina Sauce

1 cup prepared mustard
1 cup vinegar
1/4 cup ground red pepper
1/4 cup salt
1 cup water

Bring to a boil. Pour over anything that isn't moving.

Linda's KC Sauce

1 cup tomato paste
1 cup water
1/4 cup Worcestershire sauce
1/4 cup white vinegar
1/2 cup molasses
1/2 cup firmly packed brown sugar
1/4 cup onion flakes
2 tablespoons paprika
2 tablespoons celery seed
2 tablespoons salt
2 tablespoons Tabasco
2 tablespoons cracked black pepper

Combine the ingredients in the order given in a large saucepan. Stir well and simmer for about 1 hour.

Mad Dog's BBQ Sauce

1 large onion
2 tablespoons olive oil
2 tablespoons brown sugar
4 cloves garlic
2 cups tomato paste
1 cup tomato sauce
1/4 cup white vinegar
1/2 cup molasses
1/4 cup Worcestershire sauce
1 tablespoon dry mustard
1 tablespoon oregano
1 teaspoon thyme

Chip the onion fine and simmer in olive oil until transparent. Mince the garlic and add to the onion; simmer for another minute. Stir in the remaining ingredients and bring to a boil. Simmer for about 15 minutes. Store in the refrigerator. Use on any barbecue specialty.

Old-Fashioned Beer-B-Q Sauce

2 cloves garlic
2 tablespoons paprika
1 tablespoon chili powder
1 teaspoon salt
2 tablespoons soy sauce
2 tablespoons lemon juice
1/4 cup honey
1 cup tomato ketchup
1 cup tomato paste
12 ounces beer

Smash the garlic in a press or on waxed paper until well pulverized. Combine garlic, paprika, chili powder, and salt in a small bowl. Mix in the lemon juice and soy sauce; stir until blended. Add the remaining ingredients and store in a covered bowl for at least 24 hours before use. Refrigeration is recommended.

Robbie's Rib Sauce

1 cup red wine vinegar
1 cup firmly packed brown sugar
1 cup crushed pineapple
1/4 cup Madeira
1 green bell pepper, diced
1 tablespoon cornstarch dissolved in 2 tablespoons cold
    water

Combine the vinegar, sugar, pineapple, Madeira, and green
pepper in a saucepan. Bring to a boil. Add the cornstarch
and stir until clear and thickened.

Scotty's Beam Me Up Sauce

1/2 cup chopped onion
1/4 cup chopped green bell pepper
1/4 cup chopped celery
1 1/2 cups maple syrup
1/2 cup bourbon whiskey
2 tablespoons Rick's Rib Rub (page 102)
1/4 cup packed brown sugar
2 tablespoons ground black pepper
2 tablespoons salt
1 teaspoon Tabasco
1 cup tomato juice

Chop the onion, green pepper, and celery into very fine bits.
Combine with all the other ingredients in a saucepan and
simmer for about 30 minutes. Keep heat low so as not to
burn the sugars. Cool and refrigerate. Use on any barbecue
item.

Sharky's Mustard Sauce

1 tablespoon paprika
1 tablespoon ground black pepper
1 tablespoon salt
1 teaspoon garlic powder
1 cup prepared yellow mustard
1 cup packed brown sugar
1/2 cup white vinegar

Combine all the ingredients in a mixing bowl; stir until creamy. Chill for about 15 minutes before use.

Wild Bill's
Kansas City Sauce

1 cup KC Masterpiece Original Barbeque Sauce
1/2 cup Gates Original Classic Barbeque Sauce
1/4 cup white vinegar
2 tablespoons Worcestershire sauce
2 tablespoons Backyard BBQ & Grill Seasoning (page 5)

Combine all ingredients in a saucepan and simmer over medium heat for about 15 minutes. A tribute to KC's finest experts with a little spice for a kicker.

SIDE DISHES

Devilish Backyard Barbequed Eggs

24 hard-boiled eggs
1 cup prepared yellow mustard
1 teaspoon dry mustard
1 teaspoon salt
1 teaspoon paprika
1 teaspoon garlic powder
1/4 cup mayonnaise
2 tablespoons dried onion flakes

Peel and cut the eggs in half. Remove the yolks and mash them in a large mixing bowl. Place the whites on a large cookie sheet to be filled later. Combine the remaining ingredients with the egg yolks and stir well. Spoon the filling into the egg whites and chill before serving. Garnish with paprika.

Kathleen's Potato Salad

12 eggs
10 pounds russet potatoes
2 cups mayonnaise
1 cup prepared yellow mustard
1 cup diced dill pickles
1 cup sliced celery
2 tablespoons coarse black pepper
2 tablespoons salt
1/2 cup diced onion

Hard-boil the eggs, and boil the potatoes until they split. Allow the eggs and potatoes to cool, then peel and dice into small chunks. Combine all ingredients in a large mixing bowl. More mayonnaise and mustard may be added for a moist salad. Chill before serving.

Lil's Coleslaw

4 cups shredded cabbage
1/2 cup diced celery
1/2 cup shredded carrots
1/2 cup mayonnaise
1 teaspoon salt
1 tablespoon ground black pepper
1/2 cup milk
1/4 cup finely chopped onion
1 tablespoon paprika

Combine all the ingredients in a large mixing bowl. Stir
well, chill, and serve. Top with paprika and more pepper
as a garnish.

Julie's Potato Casserole

1 bag frozen shredded hash brown potatoes
1 can cream of chicken soup
1/2 cup sour cream
1/4 cup milk
2 cups grated Cheddar cheese

Mix the potatoes with the soup, sour cream, milk, and 1 cup of the grated cheese. Stir well, then spread the mixture in a 10-inch glass casserole dish. Top with the remaining cheese. Bake uncovered in a preheated 350 degree oven for 30 minutes, or until the cheese bubbles.

Smoked Pumpernickel Salad

4 small (5- or 6-inch) pumpernickel loaves
1/2 pound cooked turkey breast, diced
1/2 pound cooked ham, diced
1 small onion, minced
2 stalks celery, chopped fine
1/2 cup grated Monterey Jack cheese
1/2 cup grated Cheddar cheese
1/2 teaspoon paprika
1/2 teaspoon ground black pepper
1/2 teaspoon ground red pepper
1/2 teaspoon salt
1/4 cup mayonnaise

Slice the tops off the loaves and hollow them out, leaving a
shell about 3/4 inch thick. In a mixing bowl, combine the
turkey, ham, onion, and celery with half of each cheese.
Season with the paprika, black and red pepper, and salt.
Add the mayonnaise. Mix well and stuff the loaves with the
mixture. Top with the remainder of the cheese. Smoke, using
indirect method (see page xix), for about 1 hour or until
cheese is melted.

Jane E.'s Twice Bakes

4 large baking potatoes
1 cup grated Cheddar cheese
1 cup finely chopped mozzarella cheese
1 cup sour cream
1 tablespoon garlic powder
8 tablespoons (1 stick) butter or margarine, softened
1 tablespoon ground black pepper
1 teaspoon salt
1 tablespoon onion flakes

Bake the potatoes for 1 hour at 400 degrees. Remove from the oven and cut each potato in half lengthwise. Spoon out the insides, leaving 1/8 inch of potato on the skin. Mash the hot inside pulp with a fork. Stir in half the cheeses and all the remaining ingredients. Mix well and scoop the mixture into the potato shells; place on a baking sheet.

Put the remaining cheese in a plastic bag and shake well. Top the stuffed potatoes with the cheese and bake for 30 to 45 minutes at 300 degrees, or until cheese melts.

Heartland Bar-B-Cue Beans

2 quarts pork and beans, canned or homemade
1/4 cup Backyard BBQ & Grill Seasoning (page 5)
1/2 cup prepared yellow mustard
1 cup Heartland Bar-B-Cue Sauce (purchased)
1 onion
1 cup brisket burnt ends

In a large pan, combine the beans, seasoning, mustard, and sauce. Finely chop the onion and brisket burnt ends and stir into the beans. Place the pan in a smoker or on a grill, and smoke uncovered for 2 to 4 hours, using hickory wood.

Not
So Burnt
Endings

DESSERTS

Barbecued Bananas

4 tablespoons butter or margarine, softened
1/4 cup packed brown sugar
1/4 cup rum
2 tablespoons lemon juice
4 bananas, peeled

Coat four 12-inch squares of aluminum foil with the butter. Mix the brown sugar, rum, and lemon juice in a small dish. Coat each banana with the rum mixture and wrap tightly in foil. Place on the grill for 15 to 20 minutes.

Becerro's Kicker

1 large scoop coffee ice cream
1 1/2 ounces Kahlúa
1 1/2 ounces vodka
2 tablespoons half-and-half
2 tablespoons whipped cream
1 teaspoon shaved chocolate

Combine the ice cream, Kahlúa, vodka, and half-and-half in a blender. Mix until the consistency of a milkshake. Add more half-and-half if necessary. Pour into frosted juice or rocks glasses. Top with whipped cream and chocolate shavings.

Chilled Fruits in Wine Sauce

1 cup white wine
1/4 cup sugar
2 tablespoons lime juice
1 cup cantaloupe balls
1 cup watermelon balls
1 cup strawberries
1 cup green grapes
1 cup banana slices
6 teaspoons confectioners' sugar

Mix the wine, sugar, and lime juice in a small dish. Divide the fruit among 6 stemmed glasses and freeze for about 20 minutes. Pour the wine sauce over the fruit and top each dessert with 1 teaspoon of confectioners' sugar.

Dancing Angel Food Lemon Cake

1 angel food cake, your favorite
1 cup lemon juice
2 tablespoons amaretto
2 tablespoons vodka
1/2 cup confectioners' sugar

Set the cake on a serving dish. Make a glaze with lemon juice, amaretto, vodka, and sugar. Drizzle over the cake and chill. Serve and you'll be dancing for dessert.

Flaming Cherry Cheesecake

1 cheesecake, your favorite
1 can cherry pie filling
1/4 cup amaretto
1 tablespoon cinnamon
1 teaspoon ground ginger
2 tablespoons kirsch
1/4 cup Bacardi 151-proof rum

Prepare your favorite cheesecake, or buy one at the store. Combine the cherries, amaretto, cinnamon, and ginger in a saucepan and bring to a simmer. When warm, place the mixture in a large flat glass dish. Warm the rum in a saucepan or in the microwave. Pour the rum over the cherries and ignite. Present and serve while flaming.

Grilled Ice Cream

1/2 cup chocolate syrup
2 tablespoons Kahlúa
2 tablespoons Frangelico
1/4 cup chocolate liqueur
1/4 cup confectioners' sugar
1 quart vanilla ice cream

Mix the chocolate syrup, liqueurs, and sugar in a small bowl. Scoop the ice cream into stoneware dishes and top with the chocolate mixture, coating the ice cream evenly. Freeze for about 2 hours.

Shortly before you want to serve, place dishes on a cookie sheet and put in a covered grill until the ice cream begins to melt. Serve immediately. With a hot fire, 2 to 3 minutes is enough time on the grill.

Strawberries à la Ralph

1 quart fresh strawberries, stemmed
2 tablespoons amaretto
2 tablespoons vodka
1/4 cup confectioners' sugar
2 tablespoons Grand Marnier
2 tablespoons Bacardi 151-proof rum

Put the strawberries in one layer on a plate or baking pan and chill for about 30 minutes in the freezer. Mix the amaretto, vodka, and powdered sugar in a small dish. Add Grand Marnier and chill. Warm the rum in a microwave. Place the strawberries in chilled dishes; top with the amaretto mixture. Top again with rum and ignite. Serve flaming.

Index